1981

PERSPECTIVES ON DEATH AND DYING Series **2**

CARING RELATIONSHIPS:
The Dying and the Bereaved

EDITED BY
RICHARD A. KALISH

Baywood Publishing Company, Inc.

Library of Congress Catalog Card Number: 78-67761

ISBN Number: 0-89503-010-1

Library of Congress Cataloging in Publication Data
Main entry under title:

Caring relationships: the dying and the bereaved

(Perspectives on death in human experience series ; 2)
Includes bibliographical references.
1. Terminal care. 2. Death--Psychological aspects.
3. Bereavement. I. Kalish, Richard A. II. Series.
[DNLM: 1. Death--Collected works. 2. Attitude to
death--Collected works. 3. Terminal care--Collected
works. BF789.D4 C277]
R726.8.C38 1979   616   76-67761
ISBN 0-89503-010-1

Preface

In 1949, books and articles and films and discussion concerning death, dying, and bereavement were almost non-existent. A sociologist here, a psychiatrist there, did write about the topic or talked with a small group, but their efforts were primarily ignored. In 1959, Herman Feifel published THE MEANING OF DEATH (McGrawHill), a collection of articles on death, and the death awareness movement had its first landmark publication. In 1969, Elisabeth Kübler-Ross published ON DEATH AND DYING (Macmillan), and the death awareness movement had its guru, its charismatic leader for the following decade. By 1979, the number of books on death and dying, on helping the dying and the bereaved, on helping the helpers of the dying and bereaved, had become so great that no biblography could contain them all. And the articles, research, description, case studies, program descriptions, theory, were at least as numerous as the books. There were also the television shows, the newspaper accounts, the magazine articles, the speakers and workshops and formal classes and informal classes.

Death has "arrived." In a cynical mood, sociologist Robert Fulton once quipped "On death you can make a good living." Now that people are talking and writing so much about caring for the dying, the natural conclusion is that the dying are being better cared for. I believe that this is happening, but I also believe that the rhetoric, the words and the ideas, are moving much more rapidly than the actual quality of care. Virtually all health caretakers have read, seen, heard, or at least heard about Elisabeth Kübler-Ross, but putting new knowledge and awareness into action in institutional settings is another matter altogether.

It is easy to sit in a classroom or a lecture hall, to read a book or view a film, and to advocate the most sophisticated care procedures for being with and working with dying persons and their families. It is quite another matter to transplant these procedures into the real world. The demands of being a professional or a family member or friend in relating to a dying person are great. Sitting in a hospital room, holding your friend's hand, watching his movements, seeing her wasted body . . . this is very different than talking about what you would do if . . . .

Yet almost all of us will eventually be called on for a caring relationship with someone who is dying or someone who has lost a close friend or family member to death. It occurs more frequently for older persons, but it occurs for virtually everyone. There are some things you can do that can make you feel better about yourself in such situations, since many of us feel not only uncomfortable but angry, guilty, frightened, and impotent.

This volume brings together the writings of a number of experts working with the dying. Their chapters include the personal experiences of the mother of a dying infant and a statistical analysis of survey data of physician attitudes; theory is not ignored, but the emphasis is on experiences, ideas, and relationships. Especially relationships, since this concern provides the focus for the entire book.

Richard A. Kalish
Berkeley, California
May, 1979

Dying Man

What are they afraid of?
They make such a fuss
I no longer fear to die
The burden of my ills
has grown too much
    family
    friends
    nurses
Most of all the doctor
Why should a doctor avert his eye?
I'm not a child
I know what they signify
    the dull
    the ache
    the drag

His bite
grows greater
day by night
I see the name in their
    gesture
    manner
    step
For a meaning to life
bring the name out

        death.

Morton Leeds

Table of Contents

INTRODUCTION
Toward Standards
of Care for
the Terminally Ill

Robert J. Kastenbaum

THAT A NEED EXISTS

Who among us is satisfied with the level of care provided to the terminally ill person in the United States? It cannot be very many, judging from what this writer has had the opportunity to see and hear. We seem to be engaged in an endless round of persuading each other that the prevailing level of terminal care ranges from the inadequate to the intolerable. Often the clinical or research report documents what the patient has already learned from personal experience: that the dying person is isolated physically (Markson, 1970) and emotionally (Kübler-Ross, 1969), subject to a biased communication network (Glaser & Strauss, 1965) in a social context that gives low priority to the individual's personality and inner experiences (Weisman and Kastenbaum, 1968), and in a physical environment that may be deficient or even hazardous (Reynolds and Kalish, 1974). It would be easy to extend the list of critical reports, difficult to compile a counterbalancing set of findings that "all is well."

Increasingly, we see the dying person as victim—not of death *per se*, but of an imposed style of life that assaults and erodes values cherished by the individual. Evidence for this conclusion is convincing, so far as this writer is concerned. Although other types of data would be helpful to round out our knowledge, there is no reason to suspend action while waiting for the next study to be completed. Let us take it as sufficiently demonstrated that care of the terminally ill *should* be improved.

This leads, on a more positive note, to the likelihood that care of the terminally ill *can* be improved. Suggestions have already come from many sources.

Furthermore, scattered efforts to support the dying person—and his or her family—have already met with success. Granted that we have much to learn about techniques for helping the dying person with the entire spectrum of problems he confronts—yet the more systematic use of our best available knowledge would be of immediate benefit. Again, there is no compelling reason to wait for innovations and refinements. People in anguish today could be relieved by what is already known, but seldom applied. In Weisman's apt phrase, "safe conduct" through the perils of the terminal phase of life might be provided, even within the limitations of present knowledge and technique, to many who suffer pain, indignity, and despair (Weisman, 1972).

Here is where the question of *standards* arises. It appears to us that standards for care of the terminally ill do not exist in any explicit form in most settings where people, in fact, do pass through their last months, weeks, and hours. The absence of explicit standards seems to be accompanied by absence of staff dialogue—and likely by absence of systematic reflection—on what the goals of terminal care should be. Which comes first: the lack of standards, or the constellation of attitudes indicative of avoidance and neglect? However this question might be answered, in practice too often we see a situation in which the quality of terminal care is not evaluated as such. The health provider who is inclined to shrink from the demands of high level terminal care is protected in this reflex by the absence of standards that demand fulfillment.

We do not wish to exaggerate the power of standards. The existence of standards is not identical with their fulfillment. But it would seem that the formulation and adoption of appropriate standards for care of the terminally ill is a process worthy of our immediate attention. The very process of developing standards should itself generate new interest and insights. But outcome is even more important than process here. We believe that every terminal care setting should be guided by standards that are well articulated and taken seriously.

What should be the nature of these standards? Where will they come from? How can they be introduced effectively? Questions such as these will be touched upon. At present the author is working with a number of others to develop one possible set of standards. Perhaps similar efforts are being made by other individuals and groups—if so, let's share.

It seems fitting to note the cogent discussion of "Talk or Terminal Care?" offered recently by Edward F. Dobihal, Jr. (1974), president of New Haven's Hospice, Inc. Dobihal is deeply involved in the development of a facility modeled after Cicely Saunder's justly renown St. Christopher's Hospice in London, England. He defines terminal care as "the antithesis of the attitude conveyed when we say, 'There is nothing more we can do.' " His answer to the question raised in his title is that we need both more talk and more action—with the emphasis, understandably, on the latter. Constructive talk that leads to standards could also lead directly to action for improved care. Let's make a start!

WHAT STANDARDS EXIST TODAY?

The need to develop and implement standards of care for the terminally ill—and their families—is becoming increasingly evident. What follows here is a partial sharing of observations made by an international ad hoc task force as it set to work to address this problem.

The absence of explicit and recognized standards of care was noted by the group. It was decided to begin by making explicit those criteria which actually seem to be applied in many settings even though they are not officially stated in the handbook of rules and procedures. The following, then represents what a "good" death is in the typical medical facility of today, judging by the existing implicit standards.

1. The good or successful death is quite, uneventful. Nobody is disturbed. The death slips by with as little notice as possible.
2. Not too many people are around. In other words, there is no "scene." Staff does not have to adjust to the presence of family and other visitors who have their own needs and who are in various kinds of "states."
3. Leave-taking behavior is at a minimum.
4. The physician does not have to involve himself intimately in terminal care, especially as the end approaches.
5. The staff makes few technical errors throughout the entire terminal care process, and few mistakes in "etiquette."
6. Strong emphasis is given to the body, little to the personality or spirit of the terminally ill person in all that is done for or to him.
7. The person dies at the right time, i.e., after the full range of medical interventions has been tried, but before a lingering period has set in.
8. The staff is able to conclude that "We did everything we could for this patient."
9. Patient expresses gratitude for the excellent care received.
10. After patient's death, family expresses gratitude for the excellent care received.
11. Parts or components of the deceased are made available to the hospital for clinical, research or administrative purposes (i.e., via autopsy permission or organ gifts).
12. A memorial (financial) gift is made to the hospital in the name of the deceased.
13. The cost of the total terminal care process is determined to have been low or moderate: money was not wasted on a person whose life could not be "saved."

In the judgment of the task force, a "good death" by today's implicit standards would be one that embodies all or most of the preceding characteristics. These standards were considered to be unacceptable.

A FEW GUIDING PRINCIPLES

We need *standards of care for the terminally ill*. The standards implied by what is actually said and done in many situations today are unacceptable.

These points were sketched in previously. Now it is time to consider a few of the guiding principles that might be developed. We will limit attention to three propositions that have grown organically through discussions of an international task force concerned with standards of care. These are not "official" statements, but are communicated here so that others can join in the process of fashioning a more articulate, committed, and constructive approach.

The problem: Almost everything that is done (or not done) for the terminally ill person is justified as being in his best interests. This rationalization does not stand up to scrutiny. Many practices and decisions are oriented toward needs of the care-givers, administrators, and vested authorities. The needs of family members sometimes find expression under the flag of what is good for the patient, but often even this outlet is denied those whose lives are interwoven with the terminally ill individual. In such a climate, communication is far from adequate, and the needs of each person in the situation frequently are brought into mutual opposition.

The suggested guiding principle: *Patients, family, staff, and community all have legitimate needs and interests.* These should be clearly identified and expressed. Specific standards of care should be established in each realm.

Technically, perhaps, "standards of care" should refer only to the patient. But a caring orientation in the broad sense of the term is needed by everybody else as well. Legitimatizing the needs and interests of all people concerned with terminal care might be expected to make communications more honest and straightforward. In the long run, the patient will receive better care because his/her needs are not confused with the needs of others. It will be unnecessary to pretend that everybody else is concerned *only* for the patient. Where there are actual points of conflict among needs of patient, family, staff and community, these are more likely to be resolved.

The problem: Delivery of health services has become increasingly impersonal and bureaucratic. The terminally ill person often is "processed" in accordance with several systems external to himself (e.g., provisions of insurance plans, hospital regulations, professional habits). The details of his physical care may or may not be first-rate. But it is seldom that the personality and distincitive needs of the terminally ill person himself are offered the opportunity for expression in this process.

The suggested guiding principle: *The terminally ill person's own framework of values, preferences, and life-outlook must be taken into account in planning and conducting treatment.*

This is a standard which, in effect, maintains that treatment should *not* be standard. By recognizing individuality and encouraging its expression we will have a consistency of general approach coupled with a rich variety of person-oriented care plans. The terminally ill person him/herself would not be seen as an intrusion. Instead, there would be the expectation on all parts that the treatment plan would truly center on the unique individual. We would not expect the individual automatically to adjust to "the system."

An ambitious principle, this. It has many implications for the details of care and for the equilibrium of the care-givers. Even those who might agree with this principle *as* principle might find themselves resisting it in practice. Yet it is doubtful that specific standards of care can be effectively formulated and implemented unless there is a commitment to the individuality of the terminally ill person.

The problem: A rural area. A big city. People who have lived for generations within a close-knit ethnic enclave. People who function as part of a larger, more open society. An institution that is essentially medical in character. An institution that essentially represents the embodiment of a religious faith, with health care services only one part of the whole. These are a few of the ways in which peoples, places, and environments can be seen to differ from each other. Isn't it unrealistic to expect diverse situations to accept identical standards of care for the terminally ill when their standards for life in general may differ appreciably?

The suggested guiding principle: *Detailed standards of care should be developed in each setting to represent most adequately the fundamental values and needs, or the most compelling "vision", of the group.*

In other words, it is neither necessary nor desirable to hand down a detailed set of standards from some source on high to every situation where people are prepared to care for the terminally ill. There will be important guiding principles in common. Many of the specific standards and means of implementation may also be similar. But there must be opportunity for the distinctive character of peoples and places to enter into the development of standards of care, just as the distinctive character of each individual merits its recognition.

Consider hospices, for example. The hospice is only one of many possible settings in which care is provided for the terminally ill. But even within this type of setting, is it necessary that each hospice pursue the identical standards and aims? Or would our society be more enriched—and the options for terminally ill individuals and their families increased—if each hospice clearly outlined objectives growing out of the specific realities and values that distinguish their existence?

Guiding principles are not standards. And standards are not the same as accomplishments. But if we can find enough core agreement at this general level, perhaps we are ready to move on to the challenges of a systematic approach to terminal care that respects differences and cherishes individuality.

BIBLIOGRAPHY

Dobihal, E. F. Talk of terminal care?*Conn. Med.*, 1974, 38, 364-367.
Glaser, B. G., & Strauss, A. L. *Awareness of dying*. Chicago: Aldine Pub. Co., 1965.

Kübler-Ross, E. *On death and dying.* NY: Macmillan, 1969.

Markson, E. The geriatric house of death: Hiding the dying elder in a mental hospital. *Int. J. Aging & Hum. Develop.,* 1970, 1, 37-50.

Reynolds, D. K., & Kalish, R. A. The social ecology of dying: Observations of wards for the terminally ill. *Hosp. & Comm. Psychiat.,* 1974, 25, 147-152.

Weisman, A. D. *On dying and denying.* NY: Behavioral Publications, 1972.

Weisman, A. D., & Kastenbaum, R. *The Psychological autopsy: A study of the terminal phase of life.* NY: Behavioral Publications, 1968.

PART 1
Relationships
with
the Dying

Many people have noted that "we begin to die the moment we begin to live" and that "to live is to die." I certainly agree with these statements philosophically, but I have some problems with them when I put on my psychologist's hat. Primarily, I see them as ways to avoid the very real impact of dying for those persons whose death has become foreseeable and predictable, as well as for their family members and friends. By saying that "we are all dying", we attempt to take the sting out of death. What we do instead is to deny that death stings.

I'd like to turn the expressions around a bit. How about "we begin to live the moment we begin to die" and "to die is to live?" The first statement now suggests that an individual must confront the reality of his or her own death in order to be freed to live life to the fullest. The latter statement proposes that we all live until the moment of death, that "dying" is an adjective that describes a set of circumstances faced by a living individual.

I believe that these statements, turned around as I have done, provide significant ideas for people concerned with caring relationships, particularly for those whose caring relationships often—or even occasionally—include the dying individual (or, as Mansell Pattison has said, an individual in the living-dying interval). And this is true whether our relationship is professional or personal, whether it is loving or detached or even mildly disliking, whether it has a long history and potential future or no history and no future.

7

The following chapters emphasize the humanity of the dying person. And they also emphasize how easily that humanity can be destroyed, how vulnerable the dying and their family members are. Sometimes, as Leeds' poem says, the dying individual is ready—more than ready—for his death; sometimes, as the Koenig, Share, and Nash chapters suggest, the dying can be isolated from the not-yet-dying, to the detriment of all concerned; sometimes, as Bowie so expressively reminds us, the technology of caretaking can interfere with the humanity of those involved.

How should the dying be cared for? The answer is simple and carrying out the answer is immensely complex. Since the dying are still living, they should be cared for just like any other living person. A living person needs food and sleep and temperature regulation; he or she requires safety and security, love, self-esteem, an opportunity for personal growth. (Or, if you prefer another system of human needs, rather than Maslow's, just substitute yours for mine.) The complexity arises because satisfying the needs when a person is dying may differ: the situation is different, the feelings of those concerned are different, the time constraints are different.

Can a dying person really continue with personal growth? Of course. A dying person is a living person whose existence is bounded by the knowledge that death is probably closer in time than for most people. But growth can come through crises, through pain and suffering, through loss. In fact, I suspect that growth comes much more readily through pain than through pleasure, much more readily through failure than through success.

I'm not suggesting that we should encourage suffering in order to facilitate growth. I am suggesting that growth is possible, even in someone who is defined as dying. I would add that growth does not occur because someone, either the dying person or someone else, decides that "growth should occur." Growth or pleasure or satisfaction will develop from the situation . . . or it won't develop. Your role as a caring person is to try to set up a situation in which growth can occur, then to permit the dying person to grow or not as he or she chooses.

I believe that the possibility for growth is greatest when communication is open, when more essential needs have been met, and when human relationships are warm and caring. I also believe that there are times when this is impossible to arrange and that there are times when the needs of the specific individual will run contrary to the principles I have just espoused. In the final analysis, what most of us want most of all—when we are not hungry or in great pain—is someone who cares for us and who we know will not abandon us. And this statement too has exceptions.

CHAPTER
2

Dying vs. Well-Being[1]

Ronald Koenig

Death is frequently neither the most important nor the most difficult issue that troubles the fatally ill. They are confronted with the assault of disease on their lives, and their concerns are shaped by issues related to their deteriorating health. In the dizzying blur of tests, symptoms, procedures, and therapies, a patient often cannot see clearly the approach of his terminal moment. What he can see with clarity is how far he has come from his former state of well-being.

This distinction is important; patients with chronic fatal diseases such as cancer do not so much approach their death; they encounter the loss of their life as a function of the progression of their disease. The implications of this distinction influence the interaction between dying patients and the doctors, nurses, clergymen, social workers, etc. who attempt to help them traverse the period of their final illness.

Perhaps the young and healthy think of death as having the qualities of a thief who comes by stealth to snatch away life in the midst of its productivity and promise. It is as if the "me" who will die is the "me" I know myself to be *today*. But it is the exception when death comes as a result of an unexpected catastrophe. More often, death is the outcome of a long and difficult struggle with a disease that generates first one unpleasant variety of refractory symptoms, then another. These impositions diminish and adulterate the quality of day-to-day experience until there is little that can be relished or enjoyed and there is little hope that the balance can be returned even to a tolerable level of comfort. One's life shifts towards an illness context, and the capacity to function up to one's own standards as worker, parent, spouse, etc., is compromised.

[1] Supported in part by Clinical Cancer Training Grant T12CA08096, National Cancer Institute, U.S. Department of H.E.W.

9

PRESERVING A VIABLE QUALITY OF LIFE

In this view the primary concern of all medically related services is the preservation of a state of functional well-being that, by the standards of each individual patient, is sufficient to justify his continued life. The question is not how long a patient shall live. The question becomes: What level of well-being is compatible with continued life for *this* patient?

We must first understand what factors are essential to the patient, *by his own criteria*, for the maintenance of an acceptable quality of life. These criteria are derived from an understanding of the patient's current situation. For example, a young woman with children may be willing to allow her life to be compromised by the advancing symptoms of her disease far more than a widow in her seventies whose lesser responsibilities do not cause her to "keep fighting."

A second area related to quality-of-life has to do with the patient's potential to readjust his functional criteria to accommodate the advance of his illness. Some clues about his ability to do so derive from an understanding of past successes and failures in the patient's life. A patient who insists that life would be empty if he does not regain the use of his legs may find he can enjoy much of his life confined to a wheel chair, and may persist in relishing his life, though bedridden. Some resources, such as loving family relationships or religious faith, may not erode with advancing disease and they may continue to support and reassure patients through difficult times of sickness.

An important skill of those who work with fatally ill patients is the talent to "let people down easy" between these plateaus of increasing debility. It is at these turns-for-the-worst that the patient most needs an encouraging, supportive ally to help him go on. It is precisely at these times when physicians and other therapists find they must deal with a sense of personal failure and their own disappointment makes an encouraging demeanor sometimes difficult to find.

At these points in cancer, when metastases invade a new system, for example, one feels the approach of death and it is difficult to find encouraging words for the patient. But the patient has a different perspective. It is not the cluster of snowball blurs on his chest X-ray that define his situation but, primarily, his inability to mow the lawn or to walk up stairs. These are difficult times for the patient and his therapist. Often it is possible to offer realistic encouragement that symptoms (nausea, pain, etc.) can be controlled or made to abate when life cannot be extended. An enthusiastic effort to control symptoms and keep the patient comfortable can offer a double benefit in that he does not feel that he has become a "hopeless case." An overzealous medical commitment to the idea of cure can produce a feeling of failure when treatments are ineffective. The patient may acquire from his doctors this feeling of failure and interpret that to mean that he is not as worthwhile. He becomes sadder as he becomes sicker.

Death is not the most threatening issue to be dealt with in caring for the fatally ill. We can all imagine situations when death would be a welcome visitor.

Pain is a much-studied though not well-understood phenomenon. It is probable that each person has a tolerance beyond which he would prefer death. Before we can help with emotional stresses that may attend a patient's dying, it is necessary to control his pain. Persistent severe pain leaves one an easy victim of anxiety, depression, and anger. Success in controlling symptoms opens new and more subtle avenues for helping patients.

It is evident from examining suicide data from those who are not sick that, for many people, there is a threshold of emotional pain beyond which death is preferable. The affronts of advancing disease can generate this degree of emotional pain. A close, trusting, and supportive relationship can soothe the pain of anxiety and stem the ominous advance of depression when other analgesics have lost their salutary effect. When the patient begins to despair that he is a hopeless case, the relationship with his therapist can be a source of comfort and reassurance. This reassurance cannot occur when the patient is held at arms' length. A close relationship can affirm for him that, though he may be losing his life, he has not lost his membership among mankind. The ultimate emotional pain, despair, is less likely to occur when the relationship communicates that he is a valuable person, that his worth as a patient and a person is not predicated on the potential for remission or cure of his disease.

There is a threshold of dependency beyond which one would prefer not to live. This threshold varies widely among people, so that one may feel, "If I can't take care of myself, I don't want to go on living" [1]. Another patient may find life tolerable though quadriplegic. Even when family relationships are warm and loving, it may be difficult to persuade the patient who has been self-sufficient that his family members feel more useful and at ease when they can actively care for him. It is common for people to invest considerable importance in their ability to give to others and to measure their personal worth on their capacity to do their share, particularly in relationship with those they love. To be one who exclusively receives the attention and kindness of others is, for some, intolerable. The awareness of love increases with its expression. When the helping efforts of loving family and friends are interpreted as an expression of love, their care loses the demeaning quality of dependency. To be lovingly cared *for* may be comforting; to be taken care *of* may be demeaning.

Perhaps there is a degree of mutilation, too, beyond which one would choose to die. Though suicide among cancer patients seems relatively infrequent [2], and available data are sparse, those who do kill themselves seem most often to be patients suffering from painful and disfiguring cancer of the head and neck. Some patients with cancer refuse chemotherapy because it would cause them to lose their hair. Others allow their surgeon to dismantle their body piecemeal. Patients who have placed great importance on their physical appearance are less tolerant of the disfiguring effects of disease. This is particularly true when one feels that the security of their love relationships are dependent on sexual attractiveness. Women who experience mastectomy commonly encounter severe depression, feeling that the loss of their breast threatens the loss of their female identity. Disfiguring surgery or extreme weight loss does not escape the patient's observation. The mirror may be a more frank communication of the state of things than intricate laboratory findings.

There is also a degree of isolation and loneliness past which one might prefer death. In the course of a progressive fatal disease, patients often get caught up in the medical system, and their freedom is taken up with long periods of regular therapies and sometimes extended hospitalizations. With increased isolation from one's family members and former life, a patient may encounter a feeling of the loss of mastery over his life. Increasingly, his day-to-day activities, decisions, and sometimes his survival, are contingent on medical issues. For those who have preferred a sense of personal control and mastery over the events of their lives, the isolation and depersonalizing hospital routine can prove intolerable. Some may simply break clinic appointments and stop taking medicine. Others postpone hospitalization too long or demand that even complicated treatments be carried on while out of the hospital. Unable to work, go bowling or to church, caught up in regular visits to the doctor and "medicine every four hours," people become isolated from their former life and from many of those who populated it.

NEW PROBLEMS, OLD PROBLEMS

The most noxious effects of fatal illness are those which are most apparent to the patient. To be in pain, dependent, to become repugnant to look at and, in a state of isolation from one's family, to lose the authority to influence the course of one's own life—these exigencies can be more threatening than death. It is not that these sequelae of progressive disease *separately* affect the lives of patients. One patient may be deeply disturbed by the intrusion of one problem—pain, for example, or perhaps dependency—and unconcerned about others that are also existent. Each patient orders the problems of disease according to his own priorities. The abatement of one unfortunate difficulty may give ascendancy to the next. Often the patient's difficulties, like the medical problems of progressive disease, occur together and in tandem.

It has been observed that many patients seem to become withdrawn and appear to lose interest in their surroundings and their family, even in their illness, in the last few days or weeks of life. It seems not so much a state of serenity as apathy. Kubler-Ross and others have referred to this as a "stage of acceptance" [3]. It appears, however, to be more akin to a state of bankruptcy: a period when there are no more important credits to be added and nothing of importance left to be taken away. The patient cannot, will not, participate in the accommodation of further indignities from his disease. The therapeutic and palliative challenge is to postpone this bankruptcy at least until death is at hand.

Although there are no therapies left to try, at this point, careful attention to nursing care, unflagging interest in relieving discomfort, and close, soothing, reliable relationships can do much to relieve the terminal suffering of a patient.

There is more to be considered than those difficulties generated by advancing disease and the prospect of dying. All of the problems and conflicts that have been indigenous to a patient's life continue and, sometimes, increase during the course of one's last illness. It is not as if we can "clear the decks for death," and singularly address ourselves to the problems precipitated by illness. Old problems and conflicts remain and are often exacerbated by advancing disease. Unhappy family relationships do not resolve, but frequently deteriorate further. Alcoholic patients continue to drink, and the troubles of a fatal illness are superimposed upon more familiar problems of a patient's life. Often these old problems arise with renewed intensity to compromise a patient's comfort. Skillful and subtle understanding is necessary if we are to help guide the patient around these shoals. Broad encouragement and blanket reassurance will not do. Emotional support must derive from an understanding of past and current troubles and must be individually tailored to meet the separate needs of each patient. Habitual mechanisms of emotional defense, which have been a problematic part of the patient's neurotic interaction with others, continue to be employed and remain, as before, ineffective.

Example

Mrs. R.W., a fifty-one-year-old lady with thyroid cancer experienced an encouraging improvement in her symptoms after a course of X-ray therapy. When she entered the hospital, she was almost unable to breathe; by the time she was ready for discharge her tumors were barely palpable. When advised that her discharge was eminent, she became most apprehensive. She offered a variety of new complaints and flimsy reasons why she could not go home. . . . She was not strong enough yet—Her husband was going to a convention in Chicago, etc.

Later, in a conference with her doctor, her husband said that his main concern was how much the illness would cost him now with the regression of her cancer. He feared that health insurance coverage would run out, leaving him with massive medical bills. He said frankly that he had not felt a single affectionate emotion toward her in the last twenty years and that both of their adult children felt similarly. She had always been whiny and demanding, but he had provided for her and would continue to do so as long as he could afford it. He commented that her parents had not wanted her either, and she had been raised by a maiden aunt who was as unpleasant as she.

A later conversation with the patient went as follows:

Counselor:	I spoke with your husband; he said that he would arrange to have your son and daughter look in on you often during the three days he will be in Chicago.
Mrs. W.:	I don't know how I'll get along, what if I get sick? I live so far out! Why can't I stay here?
Counselor:	You have improved a lot. The tumors in your neck have shrunk—but you seem to feel as if you are about to be abandoned.
Mrs. W.:	What do you mean?
Counselor:	It seems to be frightening for you to leave the hospital. Let me tell you something about the program here. The treatments helped to shrink your neck tumors. While there are some tumors left, they are not causing you trouble now. We will continue to care for you when you need help. New symptoms may crop up to trouble you and we will continue to do the best we can to help with each problem as long as you need care.
Mrs. W.:	You mean there is hope for me?
Counselor:	What do you hope for?
Mrs. W.:	Well, I hope to be able to feel good. To take care of my house for a while and spend some time with my children, especially my daughter and grandson.
Counselor:	Yes, I think you will be able to do that.

The hope she needed was not the hope that she would be cured. With this patient, it was not the prospect of death which was most frightening, but a more familiar phantom in her life, the fear that she would be abandoned.

We should not expect that old problems, which are the common currency of conflict in the lives of patients (and people), can be solved. They should be circumvented. The painful process of confrontation, which is the stuff that insight-oriented psychotherapy is made of, rarely is appropriate or realistic in the counseling of patients with fatal illnesses. There is neither the energy nor the luxury of time to engage the patient in extended painful reflections about his past life difficulties. To resurrect old painful crises and expose neurotic defenses and patterns of interaction is frequently to call the patient's attention to the disappointments and failures of his life. To do so is not appropriate even though they may employ these mechanisms to their detriment in dealing with the crises of their disease. It is important for the counselor to be aware of these issues so his support can be strategically calculated to prop up just those vulnerable parts of the patient's emotional life.

THE PATIENT AS A DYING PATIENT

The recurrent issues that regularly trouble a patient are not obscure or concealed. With good rapport, most patients reveal the basic issues of conflict in an hour's conversation. With one patient it may be a fear of abandonment; with another, the loss of control over his fate; and with a third, it may be the loss of self-respect resulting from increased dependency. When these fears are persistent and severe, it is often because the life experiences of the patient have added special importance to these issues. All of this is important in understanding how each individual views his fatal illness through the lens of his past life. It is helpful to understand this view when encouraging patients to accommodate the unfortunate progression of their disease without despair. To know the inner strengths and family resources which have borne him through earlier crises in his life may provide clues to the support available to him during the course of his fatal illness.

While the prospect of death is a thing to be reckoned with that can generate a sense of desperation in some patients, such a reaction is surprisingly rare. This may be in concert with the finding that cancer patients who are aware of their diagnosis do not often report that they experience suicidal ideas [2]. A patient's life may threaten to become too shabby and tattered to enjoy. When death is regarded as fluid and situational, rather than primarily time-oriented, a different perspective of the dying experience emerges. It is less a question of how short or how long one will live, as it is how easy or difficult living will become.

This perspective spares the sick person the identity, "dying patient." Often when a patient is defined as "terminal," "incurable," or even just "dying," family, friends and medical personnel relate to him in a different way [4] —a way which further compromises his potential to finish his life with agreeable and rich experiences. Many truly gratifying things, particularly in the life of ill people, derive from their relationships with others. When those others are secretly asking themselves "I wonder what poor Charlie is thinking?" and answering "He must be thinking about being dead," there is little room for spontaneity; conversations become stilted, superficial, and narrow. When a patient acquires this dying identity in the eyes of his fellows, they become uneasy talking with him about the more distant future, about crises and problems at home, current troubles on his old job and even problems of his illness that might reach beyond a patronizing, "How are you doing today?"

HOPE AND HOPELESS CASES

In this time-bound notion of death, dying is treated as a kind of failure. It is concealed in nursing homes and, if death is anticipated, in the private rooms of hospitals. At one hospital, when there are no further therapeutic modalities to be tried the patient who was formerly a "Melanoma" or a "Hodgkin's" becomes a "T.L.C."; the operational definition of a "T.L.C." is a negative one. No "code blue" or cardiac arrest team is called; no antibiotics, or respirators, are used. The needs of the staff and patient may *both* be best met if the patient dies soon when no other therapy is appropriate. But the patient should be made comfortable; he should not become further isolated. Tender-Loving-Care, to be such, must include increased contact and interest in caring *about* the patient. There are no patients who are so miserable that they are beyond all help.

Patients who are dying are especially receptive to overt affection and the attentive ministrations of hospital staff. Touching is important. Sick people, the elderly, and children are receptive to touch. Stroking is natural and well understood as a source of comfort. When one is sick, these kinds of interaction may have more effect than verbal reassurances. Even when specific treatment is not possible, one may enjoy considerable benefit from talking with his therapist, perhaps by the same mechanism which enables patients to benefit from placebos. The *experience* of being cared for may benefit the patient more than the direct effect of the care. It is much more satisfying to the staff, nurses, doctors, etc. when they feel there is something they can do which seems to help the patient feel better. When other analgesics lose their potency, the relationship continues as a soothing source of comfort. The most commonly reported work-related stress of cancer nurses is the frustration of feeling there is nothing more they can do to help.

Approaching the dying patient from the perspective that the current situation is of central importance, and that the idea of dying is secondary, influences the transactions between staff and patient. If we believe that the patient is troubled mainly by anxieties about annihilation, nonexistence, about being dead, then our hands are tied. There is little honest encouragement we can offer because death is inevitable. Even in order to devise helpful strategies we must reach beyond the notion, "Of course she is anxious; she is dying," and toward the idea "I can understand why this patient is anxious, and I can help her to resolve her fears." A state of chronic depression or of anxiety is not common or "natural" for dying patients [5]. Particularly at the outset, when the fatal diagnosis has only just been confirmed, it is a helpful perspective from which to talk to patients. Then the question is posed: "What can I say to this patient when there is no hope?" If hope is synonymous with cure, then despair is synonymous with death. In fact, many people do not expect to live forever; nor, do they hope to get out of life alive. In the context of this perspective a discussion with a patient recently diagnosed to have a fatal disease might go as follows [6]:

> "You have one of those diseases for which we have no cure. Although we can't cure this illness, we know quite a bit about it and there is an arsenal of treatments which have often proved to be effective in controlling it, sometimes for a long time. I can't be sure how you will react to these treatments. We have to try some and see how they work. I will let you know how things are going as we go along. Eventually these treatments (chemotherapy, radiation, surgery, etc.) will become less and less effective and will no longer control the disease, but I cannot say when that will happen. You are likely to have extended periods of time when you will feel well and can go about life as usual. From time to time you will have to come in for further treatment. You may have some trouble with symptoms like nausea, pain, etc., but we can control these if we work together. You will be comfortable. Whatever troubles come up, I will be available to help work them out."

Such an approach is both honest and reassuring. To hedge or minimize the situation is to be caught in a lie by the natural course of the disease. To be vague is to appear not to understand the patient's problem. Sometimes patients or family press for more specific information about the prospects of their death with questions such as "All right, I want to know how long I've got." To give a patient a definite death date, whenever it may be, is dishonest. No one can, with certainty, predict a patient's death, and to do so rarely makes him feel better. The maintenance of a solid relationship of trust demands, however, that the question be answered. If the therapist is aware that the patient understands his disease, a frank answer to a patient with lung cancer for example, might proceed in this fashion [6]:

> "You understand that you are in a dangerous situation so far as your illness is concerned. I cannot be sure how much or how long, our treatment will help. You are not in danger of dying right now and I don't think you will be soon, but, because this is a dangerous illness, you should try to plan for the worst so that even if things go badly you will be prepared. You wouldn't like to have to take care of important business when you feel sick. You are not a statistic and each person is different but this is a difficult disease. Only about one out of ten people live more than a year after it has been diagnosed. That one patient, however, may go on feeling good for two or three or more years. We will keep working with you whatever comes up to try to keep you feeling good and solve whatever problems you run into."

DENIAL, ACCEPTANCE, AND STRATEGIC REASSURANCE

Often patients have an idea that something is seriously wrong before they go to the doctor. Even when patients have not expected to hear that they have a fatal disease, the state of shock and bewilderment of learning they may soon die does not last long [7]. Within a few days, perhaps a month, most patients seem to push the full awareness from their consciousness. Some have called this denial, a term that has much ambiguity. If the symptoms of disease develop slowly over weeks or months, the prospect of death soon regains a quality of uncertainty and this uncertainty seems to bring reassurance with it. The patient who formerly expected to live twenty or twenty-five years now expects to live two, three, or four years. It is difficult to anticipate the general future in a tangible way. Often it is disappointing to lose the prospect of an extended future, but patients usually accommodate the change to a shortened, though still uncertain future, without chronic depression or persistent anxiety.

We can only anticipate the future and remember the past, but the time one really lives is on the crest of the immediate present. Many patients say, "I take one day at a time. I try to enjoy each day as much as I can and not worry about anything else." As an attitudinal coping mechanism this orientation to the immediate situation, today, seems to be widely and effectively used by dying patients. The uncertainty of the future seems to make its dismal prospect easier to ignore. This is not denial in the usual psychological sense of the word. *One does not need to deny what has not yet happened*. Though he "knows" he has a fatal disease, he may not choose to examine the potentially horrible ramifications of the future. If a patient does the things he is expected to do, and if he cooperates with his doctor and participates in his treatment, then it is not necessary for him to admit to others that he has a fatal disease. Patients confront the awareness of their situation in their own terms. To insist that they confront the issue with the awareness "I have cancer, I am dying," is often to impose someone else's terms and perspective upon them.

On the other side of the concept of denial lies the equally spongy notion of "acceptance." Some have regarded this as a kind of ethereal state of serenity. It has been advanced as the ideal attitude to take toward one's own death or, for that matter, toward any crisis. ("Lord give me the strength to accept what I cannot change," etc.) It makes little sense to encourage a patient to struggle on bravely, simply because one is expected to say encouraging things. If a patient complains incessantly and cannot seem to put this frustration or that loss out of his mind, it may be that those around him do not fully appreciate the meaning of the problem. To complain and rail against his fate may be appropriate in view of the patient's loss. Such a reaction may indicate that a patient remains concerned and involved with his life.

In maximizing the patient's capacity to find pleasure in his situation, it is important that he know when he is doing well. Many times patients are reluctant to ask questions, fearing they will hear bad news. Unless their physician volunteers the information, their reticence prevents them also from hearing favorable reports. They should be told they are doing well in the medical sense when their illness is responding to treatment, and well in the personal sense when they are behaving as a "good patient." Patients are frequently uncertain of what is expected of them and they may be playing the role of patient for the first time. A sick person gives up his role as worker, spouse, etc. and assumes the restricted role of patient. The doctor and nurse are keenly aware of the dimensions of their responsibility as they go about their work. The patient, too, should have some opportunity to take pride in his performance as he cooperates in his own care and treatment. Acceptance of the role of patient, as well as "acceptance" of one's disability, is measured by behavior regarded as *acceptable* by the staff and family. The patient benefits if there is a wide range of behavior considered acceptable, and if he understands what is appropriate patient behavior.

The same kind of reassurance—"You are doing a good job in a difficult situation"—can be directed toward family members when they are feeling the grinding responsibility of caring for the patient at home. It makes sense to be explicit with people about their behavior; i.e., "I admire the strength you are showing in dealing with the hard problems of this sickness. You are doing a good job!"

COMMUNICATION

A common concern expressed by nurses and others who work with dying patients has to do with their ability to "communicate" with their patients. They fear they will blunder, say the wrong thing, or be unable to find anything to talk about. Privately, they worry that the patient may pin them with one of those devastating questions such as, "Am I dying?" or "What is going to happen to me?" or, "How can I enjoy anything when I know I'm going to die soon?" Usually patients are more subtle and, out of consideration for their doctors and nurses, they couch their questions in less provocative terms.

The first temptation may be to try to ignore the difference between the patient's and one's own situation with a form of the reply, "We all have to die, you know. I could get killed on the way home." At best there is little reassurance in this kind of response.

These questions cannot be gently and effectively handled with sloganized replies. At these times one may be tempted to remember that he has an important coffeebreak to attend. One may fear that the kindness, sensitivity, and tact which has been the currency of his other relationships with patients will desert him now, and that the patient may crumble into a heap of despair for lack of the "right" answer. In reality, patients are rarely so fragile; and, the staff, most of whom have selected their professions out of a personal commitment to humanism, are not seized by callous insensitivity.

When the patient seems to be concerned about dying, his concern should be seen from two simultaneous perspectives. One perspective might be characterized by the statement, "I am ready to learn more about my situation so long as what you tell me is not *all* bad news." With a little thought, one can find some optimistic encouragement to mix with the most grim and disappointing reality. After initially telling a patient his diagnosis and its meaning, it is generally wise to educate a patient about his disease as things develop, a little at a time, building an alliance as symptoms and problems arise.

The second perspective, perhaps more important than the informational component, has to do with the patient's feelings about himself vis-a-vis his fatal illness. The patient's references to dying can be seen as an invitation to become more intimate. This is particularly true, when one meets a patient in the middle or late in the course of the disease, after they have been aware of their condition for some time. His concerns are likely to be about himself—and not about the "leap into eternity."

Sometimes anxious patients make reference to their death almost casually, or allude to issues about dying when there is little opportunity to take time to discuss such poignant matters. Sometimes they ask death-related questions of those whom they know are unfamiliar with their case. The patient's needs cannot be met if the counselor's response is exclusively related to his prospects in a medical sense. Some other issues need to be taken into account:

1. One should ask the patient what he already knows and suspects about his illness. Although his questions may imply that he is naive about his disease, it often becomes apparent that he is cognizant in detail of his diagnosis and prognosis. To secure a detailed understanding of the patient's perception of his situation is not an intrusion for it communicates that one is truly interested in him. We are not so concerned here in a technical explanation of his situation as in the patient's own view. This puts a question like, "Am I dying?" into a more personally relevant context, emphasizing the "I" more than the "dying." This understanding avoids repetition of medical information but, more importantly, allows the nurse, intern, social worker, etc., to avoid upsetting conflicts with basic information the patient has been given by others who are working with him. Often we need to give the patient little additional factual information when we understand what he already knows.

2. It is necessary to understand what is important to the patient about his life, his relationships, work, interests, past successes, and hopes for the future. To talk with a patient about his death we must first know about his life. It does not ordinarily require a complex psychological analysis to reach an understanding of the facets of life that are of high priority and importance to him—he will tell you about his children, travel, music, privacy, independence, etc. The possibilities are various, but they are rarely concealed. The crisis of illness brings them more sharply to his awareness as the threat of their loss is keenly felt. The meaning of the question "Am I dying?" becomes more subtle as these things are understood.

3. It is often worthwhile to ask a patient who seems concerned about death what it is about dying that he fears. Simply putting his feelings into words can diffuse much of the anxiety. Concerns about dying which he harbors may not be appropriate to his situation. He may be unnecessarily concerned that his young family will not be able to get along without him. Another patient may worry that he will finish his life in some drab and smelly nursing home. There is time for reassuring plans to be made to avoid these outcomes. Sometimes the patient may be worried about issues which, in his case, are not a real threat.

Example

Mrs. G. constantly badgered her doctors about how and when she would die. An attractive lady, 42 years old, she was married and the mother of two adolescent daughters.

Throughout the three year course of her breast cancer she had staunchly maintained her dominant position in the family. She maintained her assertiveness until bone metastases forced her to remain bedridden.

Mr. G. was worried that his wife would kill herself. He knew that she had secreted a cache of pills.

After an initial period of testing and sparring, when some rapport had developed (about one half hour), the counselor advised Mrs. G. that he was aware she had hidden some pills in order to kill herself and since that was a hard decision to make, he hoped that talking about her situation would help her to feel better and to get along better with the staff. The counselor assured her that he would not attempt to stop her if she decided to kill herself.

Dialogue

Mrs. G.:	Did the doctors tell you I'm a trouble maker? Is that why they sent you?
Counselor:	They told me that you are full of questions about your death that they can't answer. It makes them uneasy when they talk to you. I'm worried about what's going on with you to make you feel so bad that you need to plan to kill yourself.
Mrs. G.:	I have a bottle of Seconal (but I don't want you to tell anyone). I don't know how many to take, and I need to know how much time I'll need after taking them so it's too late to pump my stomach.
Counselor:	I can get the information and tell you tomorrow. You should understand that I will do this so you can feel in control of your life, not because I want you to kill yourself. Why are you thinking about killing yourself?
Mrs. G.:	My father had a stroke when I was fifteen. He was a vegetable for the next three years. I lost my adolescence taking care of him and I won't have that happen to my daughters because of me.
Counselor:	There is no danger that it will go that way for your daughters. You know you have cancer and that is very different from your father's illness. If the medicine you are taking is able to control your disease then you will, for the most part, take care of yourself. If not, you won't linger on as an invalid for a long time.

When the counselor returned the next day, Mrs. G. indicated she was pleased to see him but too tired to talk. It appeared that she no longer needed to know about the barbiturate dose. In two or three days she lapsed into a coma and died of her disease. The threat of death for this patient was far less of her concern than the danger of visiting upon her daughters the problems which she had in her own adolescent years.

CONCLUSION

The idea of dying as it has been considered by existential philosophers—that is, dying viewed as the prospect of annihilation—is only one of the many deathly visages to be examined and not commonly the dying person's concern [8]. In a qualitative sense, to die becomes a fluid and various experience; in a quantitative existential sense it becomes no experience at all. In that sense the *anticipation* of death is the only way it can be experienced for, when death happens, it is already after the fact. When death is engaged as an ongoing factor in all of the experiences of living, then strategies, can be devised to hold back dying by enriching the quality of life.

When the terminal moment arrives after a difficult, progressive fatal disease, the individual has been changed by the effects of disease upon him. The idea of dying in the context of current experience gives a different dimension to the understanding of the dying patient. This paper has dealt almost exclusively with the experience of the patient.

The hazards and troubles of illness may have mutative effects on relationships within families. It may affect the lives of those who are emotionally near the patient in different ways. It is common in the late phases of disease for adult children, or others who care about the patient, to say: "Mother has suffered enough; can't we let her die;" However one may answer that question ethically, it is evident that the relationship with the patient is different than it had been before her illness. Grieving has already begun. Sometimes the "work" of mourning may be nearly over before the patient is dead. The implications of the concept of dying-as-current-experience for bereavement may offer some fruitful insights worth further consideration. The application of such an idea to problems in gerontology and rehabilitation may also have merit.

REFERENCES

1. Koenig, R., Goldner, N. S., Kresojevich, R., and Lockwood, G. Ideas about illness of elderly black and white in an urban hospital, *Aging and Human Development*, 1971, 2, 217-225.
2. Peck, A. Emotional reactions to having cancer, *Ca-A Cancer Journal for Clinicians*, 1972, 22.
3. Kubler-Ross, E. *On Death and Dying,* New York: The Macmillan Company, 1971.
4. Glaser, B. G., and Strauss, A. L. *Awareness of Dying*, Chicago: Aldine, 1965.
5. Koenig, R., Levin, S. M., and Brennan, M. J., The emotional status of cancer patients as measured by a psychological test, *Journal of Chronic Disease*, 1968.
6. Private communication with Dr. V. K. Vatkevicius, Professor of Medicine in Oncology, Wayne State University, Detroit, Michigan.
7. Quint, J. C. Mastectomy: Symbol of cure or warning sign? In Folta, J., and Dech, E. S. (Eds.), *A Sociological Framework for Patient Care*. New York: John Wiley and Sons, 1966, 272.
8. Kastenbaum, R., and Aisenberg, R. *The Psychology of Death*, New York: Springer, 1972.

CHAPTER 3

Toward a
Social Theory
of Dying

Natalie Rosel

As an area of specialization develops, it begins to spawn subspecialties and new terminology until it is difficult to keep a perspective on the field as a whole. Such is the case with our knowledge of dying, a field with a rapidly growing literature but little to offer in the way of comprehensive frameworks. Rather than simply review this literature, or add yet another specific approach to dying, the following paper will attempt to codify existing orientations into a single framework. The purpose of this task is to make progress toward a social theory of dying.

Three dimensions of social reality appropriately serve to organize the literature. The social psychological dimension will focus on the experience of coping with loss and separation. The institutional dimension will consist of role relationships centering around the dying person and the organizational context in which these relationships exist. And the societal dimension will consider the values and attitudes which influence the practices and behavior patterns concerning those who are dying.

Dimensions of Social Reality

EFFECTIVE COPING

Many things could be categorized as losses for the dying. Physical losses, including control over one's body and life-style, are as severe in consequence as the emotional strains of diminishing self-esteem or withdrawn affections from those close to the dying, such as family and friends.

> The most noxious effects of fatal illness are those which are the most apparent to the patient. To be in pain, dependent, to become repugnant to look at and, in a state of isolation from one's family, to lose the authority to influence the course of one's own life—these exigencies can be more threatening than death [1].

Coping with these effects is a matter of attitude as well as behavior.

Effective coping with physical stress includes the ability of caretakers to make the dying person comfortable. According to Hinton, "With good care, the pain of most fatal conditions, including cancer, can usually be relieved" [2]. This same attitude of providing comfort is expressed by Saunders: "Personal, caring contact is the most important comfort we can give" [3]. Coping with pain has an important attitude dimension of caring for the dying. This dimension is as important as the technical regulation of drugs or treatment. It is assurance to the dying that their pain will be controlled, that minimizes the fear of pain and consequently the anxiety that sometimes contributes substantially to the experience of physical stress.

Coping with emotional strain is a matter of psychological reaction as well as social response. Reactions to impending separation frequently bring about awkward communication and even withdrawal on the part of those who are emotionally attached to the dying person. Grief which is unexpressed or unshared cuts off an important line of communication. The expression of fears and concerns is crucial for the dying person; it is a means of sharing a number of important feelings which might make leave-taking an easier process, to some extent replacing isolation and unexpressed grief.

The work of Kübler-Ross [4], Norton [5], and Kutscher [6], all confirm the importance of communication and the avoidance of isolation or abandonment. The importance of listening to dying persons is stressed by Kübler-Ross as is a willingness to share concerns openly whenever it is appropriate. This same receptivity is emphasized in therapeutic response of a psychoanalyst, Janice Norton, when she assures a dying woman that "I would be available to her at any time, and would be for as long as she needed me" [5].

The sharing of fears and grief alleviates the emotional strain for both the dying person and those who are close to him. The positive role of this sharing is well summarized by Kutscher.

Most patients seem to fear the process of dying more than the unknown quantity, death. Yet, if those who will mourn his death would share their feelings with him in the living *now*, if emotional *ex*pression rather than emotional *re*pression were to be allowed, many fears could be allayed; for many more, the terminal days could be a time for a kind of exquisite loving, sharing, and planning, and anticipatory grief for all would take on its most useful form and beneficent qualities [6].

Dying persons must also cope with their own awareness of death, regardless of how openly impending death is communicated [7]. (The assumption that dying persons are aware of their terminal condition whether or not they are explicitly told is usually correct.) Coping often includes an initial denial or protest, and in some cases a form of acceptance or detachment is eventually reached [4]. Coming to terms with the awareness of death is an individual matter. Sometimes a progression of stages can be observed, but this is certainly not invariably the case. When the progression is observed, there are often reactions of anger, bargaining or depression between the initial denial and the final acceptance. The point is that emotional reactions on the part of dying persons are appropriate means of coping with their awareness of death.

In addition to coping with physical and emotional stress, dying persons must cope with separation from life itself. Awareness of this necessity can facilitate the expression of emotions, and in fact provide for patterns of expectations and reinforcement. An excellent literary illustration is provided by Tolstoy's "Death of Ivan Ilych."

He saw that no one felt for him, because no one even wished to grasp his position. Only Gerasim (Ilych's servant) recognized it and pitied him. And so Ivan Ilych felt at ease only with him.

Once when Ivan Ilych was sending him away he even said straight out: "We shall all of us die, so why should I grudge a little trouble?"— expressing the fact that he did not think his work burdensome, because he was doing it for a dying man and hoped someone would do the same for him when his time came [8].

EXPECTATION AND REINFORCEMENT

Patterns of expectation and reinforcement are problematic and ill defined with respect to dying persons. Ambiguities exist for both the dying person himself and for those who interact with him. Definitions which do exist are negative, such as a physician's defining a dying person as someone he can no longer help (cure). There are no prescriptions for rituals or behavior, and thus the "marginal man" role is appropriate [9]. Some of this ambiguity can be accounted for by the institutional setting in which most people die.

The "all-American" social structure, bureaucracy, has minimized the impact of death on society, but it has failed to minimize the problems of the process of dying.

Classic studies of hospital treatment of the dying by Sudnow [10] and Glaser and Strauss [7] delineate examples of the lack of role relationships for those who are dying. In fact Sudnow characterizes a self-fulfilling prophecy whereby the dying person is responded to as if he were already dead [10]. Beyond confirming the social nature of the process of dying, these studies demonstrate the anomic situation of a setting whose goals are curing diseases, taking on the care of "uncurables." One example of effective caring for the dying is Hospice, located in England (and one beginning with out-patient services in this country). Role relationships in such settings revolve around self-determination for the dying person (the exercise of as much independence and self-reliance as possible), and pain control and the provision of companionship by the staff. The norms are the obvious ones of comfort and assistance, but more important they include the dying person as taking an active part in his own care and decision-making.

Another response is a change in our structural arrangements so that the dying person can be cared for in the home. This systemic change is proposed by Ramsey.

There is a final entailment of caring for the dying that is required of priests, ministers, rabbis, and every one of us, and not only or not even mainly of the medical profession. "The process of dying" needs to be got out of the hospitals and back into the home and in the midst of family, neighborhood and friends. This would be a "systemic change" in our present institutions for caring for the dying as difficult to bring about as some fundamental change in foreign policy or the nation-state system. Still, any doctor will tell you that by no means does everyone need to die in a hospital who today does so [11].

A study conducted in England by Cartwright, Hockey and Anderson investigated the social and medical circumstances of adults who died in 1969 [12]. Over a third of these deaths occurred in private homes, but the study documents the many difficulties of adequate care under these circumstances— difficulties which are not attributable to any lack of human support, but rather of facilities. Relatives provided most of the caretaking: wives and husbands in the case of married couples, daughters for the widowed, siblings and more distant relatives for the singles. Under these circumstances the caretaker role is added to the ongoing familial relationship, and the earlier mentioned problem of norms and expectations does not exist.

In Simone de Beauvoir's account of her mother's death in a hospital, she relates the protective feelings toward her mother and speaks of the mother-daughter relationship she experienced.

I had grown very fond of this dying woman. As we talked in the half-darkness I assuaged an old unhappiness; I was renewing the dialogue that had been broken off during my adolescence and that our differences and our likenesses had never allowed us to take up again. And the early tenderness that I had thought dead forever came to life again, since it had become possible for it to slip into simple words and actions [13].

The question being raised is whether or not new role relationships with the dying would be as effective as the continuation of existing relationships. This includes the doctor-patient relationship with its basis in care-taking instead of curing. In this context, the institutional setting in which dying occurs must be taken into account: its organizational goals, and hence its operating procedures.

Because social structures reflect societal values, it is necessary to include a still larger frame of reference for developing a comprehensive approach to dying. What attitudes do we hold as a society that affect our responses to dying?

SCIENCE'S CONQUEST

As a society, we tend to look to science and technology for solutions to problems. We do not see theological explanations as answers to problems. This historical shift is elaborated by Toynbee, who describes this change as taking place over the course of three centuries and who raises appropriate questions about its effect on attitudes toward dying.

> Human beings who are imbued with the spirit of pre-seventeenth century Western Christendom find it easier than their descendants find it to face the fact of death frankly and robustly.
> Science, applied with sensational success to technology, has substituted the physical conquest of non-human nature for the spiritual conquest of himself as Western's man's ideal paramount objective. . . . Confronted by death without belief, modern man has deliberately been clipping his spiritual wings [14].

Science means procedures of control, and modern society removes the dying to places where the handling of death is controlled through bureaucratic procedures. Discussion of this process is offered by Robert Blauner.

> When the dying are segregated among specialists for whom contact with death has become routine and even somewhat impersonal, neither their presence while alive nor as corpses interferes greatly with the mainstream of life [15].

Developing at the same time were attitudes which elevated "youth" to a position of importance and promise in society. Youth is valued by society, old age is not. Youth belongs in the limelight, old age in the shadows. Attitudes such as these reinforce our age-segregated society. Youthful people are highly visible and older members less so. In the words of Kastenbaum and Aisenberg; ". . . death is becoming detached and transposed from the valued core of society, the young." "It is an event that befalls only those people who have already become obsolete . . ." [16]. Thus, attitudes toward youth and old age also have an effect on patterns and practices concerning dying.

These two sets of attitudes provide the societal context for dying, the broad framework in which institutional procedures take place, and the value system that affects social psychological efforts to cope with dying.

SOCIALIZATION

Socialization, the process by which individuals acquire the means to carry out roles in society, is a life-long process. Role prescriptions are learned in a variety of social surroundings. Not only role expectations, but also the ability to project oneself into another's position, are learned in this manner. Role learning and role-taking continue throughout the course of a lifetime: new roles are continually acquired and old ones left behind. Another dimension of socialization is anticipatory. Individuals frequently project themselves into the future and imagine themselves enacting roles that they will later occupy. Recruits into professions often do this, and to some extent it makes sense to talk about self-socialization. Regardless of the form it takes, the socialization process is the means by which individuals learn to play roles and to empathize with individuals in other positions.

In our society, there are no opportunities for socialization with respect to dying. Dying does not take place in society as a whole but rather in restricted social settings. This means that people are facing role relationships for which there is no preparation. There has been no anticipatory socialization, neither have there been opportunities for learning through projection. The restricted setting in which dying occurs restricts the natural opportunities to learn about dying. For society as a whole, the socialization process does not include the last stage of life.

The physical environment also has a great deal to do with whether or not socialization for dying occurs. Dying usually occurs in settings that have bureaucratic structures and goals that are incompatible with the process of dying. This means that the majority of institutions neither socialize those who are dying nor those who are interacting with them. Therefore, the social-psychological problems of coping are socially determined without a support system for role learning.

Individuals who are dying are at the center of a fabric of values and practices that result in ambiguity and isolation during the last stage of life. The dying and those relating to them must attempt to cope with the problems outlined above in the absence of preparation (learning) and a supportive social system.

The codification of existing approaches to dying can be realized in the application of socialization as defined in role learning.

1. There are no opportunities for anticipatory socialization with respect to dying. The values of our society in effect remove the dying members.
2. There are no opportunities for socialization within institutional settings where most dying occurs, because the goals and structures of these settings are not oriented to the process of dying.

3. In the absence of anticipatory socialization and role relationships within institutions, individuals must cope with the problems of dying (living the last stage of life) in ambiguity and often in isolation.

REFERENCES

1. R. Koenig, Dying vs. Well-Being, *Omega, 4:3*, p. 184, 1973.
2. J. Hinton, *Dying,* Penguin Books, Baltimore, 1967.
3. C. Saunders, The Moment of Truth, *Death and Dying,* L. Pearson (ed.), Case Western Reserve University, Cleveland, 1969.
4. E. Kübler-Ross, *On Death and Dying,* Macmillan, New York, 1969.
5. J. Norton, Treatment of a Dying Patient, *Death: Interpretations,* H. Ruitenbeek (ed.), Dell, New York, 1969.
6. A. Kutscher, Anticipating Grief, Death, and Bereavement A Continuium, *The Phenomenon of Death,* E. Wyschogrod (ed.), Harper and Row, New York, 1973.
7. B. Glaser and A. Strauss, *Awareness of Dying,* Aldine, Chicago, 1965.
8. L. Tolstoy, The Death of Ivan Ilych, *The Death of Ivan Ilych and Other Stories,* Signet, New York, 1960.
9. D. Crane, Dying and Its Dilemma as a Field of Research, *The Dying Patient,* O. Brim et. al., Russell Sage, New York, 1970.
10. D. Sudnow, *Passing On: The Social Organization of Dying,* Prentice-Hall, New Jersey, 1967.
11. P. Ramsey, *The Patient as Person,* Yale Universtiy Press, New Haven, p. 135, 1970.
12. A. Cartwright et. al., *Life Before Death,* Routledge and Kegan Paul, Boston, 1973.
13. S. de Beauvoir, *A Very Easy Death,* Warner, New York, p. 89, 1973.
14. A. Toynbee, Changing Attitudes Towards Death in the Modern Western World, *Man's Concern with Death,* A. Toynbee (ed.), McGraw-Hill, New York, p. 129, 1968.
15. R. Blauner, Death and Social Structure, *Psychiatry, 29,* p. 384, November, 1966.
16. R. Kastenbaum and R. Aisenberg, *The Psychology of Death,* Springer, New York, p. 206, 1972.

CHAPTER
4

Family Communication
in the Crisis of
a Child's Fatal Illness:
A Literature Review
and Analysis

Lynda Share

Probably one of the greatest crises a family can experience is the anticipated loss of a child through a catastrophic, fatal illness such as leukemia. As a major cause of childhood death in the United States, approximately 2,000 children under the age of fifteen die from leukemia annually (*Medical World News*, 1971). While prior to the 1950's, the leukemic child was likely to survive approximately four months, advances in treatment procedures have resulted in considerable prolongation of life, such that the average survival time is now two to three years. The course of the illness is still, however, extremely variable and cannot be predicted in advance. Thus, many children have a series of relapses and remissions until the ultimate terminal phase; others never achieve remission (Bozeman et al., 1955; Kaplan, 1971).

The stresses imposed by the need to watch and care for the leukemic child over a period of months, sometimes years, tax even the strongest family's adaptational resources. These stresses—chronic and severe—can activate old family conflicts, exacerbate existing tensions, and bring about long-term detrimental consequences for the integrity of the family unit and for the emotional well-being of its individual members. Thus, as Binger et al (1969) report in a retrospective study of twenty leukemic families, "In half of the families at least one member reacted so strongly to the crisis as to need psychiatric help . . . none had required such help before (p. 417)." Divorce, illness, and behavioral and school problems are also common among well children (Binger et al., 1969; Kaplan, 1971). More specifically, the illness and the threat which it implies transforms the whole texture of family life, affecting each of the family members in different ways.

For the parents, it means the loss of cherished hopes and values and affirms that their aspirations and strivings for their child were in vain. It represents an assault on the parents' self-image, particularly an assault on their role of omnipotent protector. Above all, the threatened and actual loss of their child represents a symbolic loss of self. As Natterson and Knudson (1960) state in a discussion of the mother-child relationship, "The threat of death to the child poses a symbolic threat of death to the mother . . . In a sense, the mother faces death, experiences it, and survives (p. 461)."

For the well siblings, the illness means a loss of customary parental attention, now focused on the leukemic child. During hospitalizations, it means the parents' actual physical absence, role realignments within the family, and changes in valued family activities and routines. The children must deal with a confusing array of feelings resulting from these and other consequences of the illness: anger towards the parents, increased rivalry and hostility towards the ill child—especially when he is in remission and supposedly "well"—followed by fear and often intense guilt when the leukemic child is again hospitalized (Wiener, 1970; McCollum & Schwartz, 1972).

For the leukemic child, the illness challenges at all levels his feelings of self-worth and his growing sense of autonomy and physical integrity. This is so regardless of whether or not he is aware of the fatal outcome. Thus, when the disease is active, changes in energy for physical activity take place. The ill child experiences separation from his family and familiar surroundings during periods of hospitalization and must relinquish active care of his own physical needs to medical personnel and parents. Medical procedures are numerous and often quite painful. Some drugs used to combat the disease produce a cushinoid[1] appearance and others cause total hair loss (Lyman & Burchenal, 1963). The ensuing threat to his body integrity and self-image is often magnified by the blatant comments and reactions of neighborhood children and by the distress of significant adults in the child's environment concerning the obvious physical deformities. In addition, the chronicity of the illness, recurrent hospitalizations, death or disappearance of other hospitalized children and the emotionally charged interpersonal climate, all intensify the leukemic child's fantasies and fears and contradict what he had previously experienced as a growing ability to correctly interpret and make sense out of the happenings in the world around him.

Alleviating some of these stresses and, in a broader sense, improving the quality of life for the fatally ill child and his family have become growing concerns of the behavioral scientist and medical professional (e.g., Kalish, 1969; Kubler-Ross, 1969). Increasingly, these concerns have focused on the issue of communication: How does one communicate with the dying child about his illness so that his fears and anxieties may be lessened? What type of environment for communication within the total family would be most beneficial for its individual members? The importance of these questions for practioner, dying child, and family prompted the analysis of current literature and research which follows.

FAMILY COMMUNICATION: THE CONTROVERSY

An examination of the literature suggests two opposing answers—with numerous variations—to the above questions. We might term one answer the "protective approach", the other, the "open" or "open environment approach". Essentially, the protective approach involves the belief that the ill child and often his siblings should be shielded from knowledge of the disease diagnosis and prognosis (Plank, 1964; Toch, 1964; Agranoff & Mauer, 1965; Howell, 1966; Verwoerdt, 1966; Evans, 1968; Sigler, 1970). Parents may be encouraged to openly share with each other their feelings and concerns regarding the illness (Verwoerdt, 1966), provided this is not done in the presence of the children (Howell, 1966). This difference in handling parent-parent communication as

---

[1] An occasional side-effect of cortico-steroid treatment, cushinoid appearance involves the development of a "moon face," abdominal distention, and other visible physical changes that tend to make the patient look "different" and less attractive.

opposed to parent-child communication is rationalized on the basis of different require-ments for effective coping. Thus, for the parents, effective coping entails, among other things, accomplishing some of the grief work in advance of the child's death (e.g., Friedman et al., 1963; Hoffman & Futterman, 1971)—a task which proponents of both the protective and open views see as facilitated by parents' mutual expression of feelings and provision of support (Verwoerdt, 1966; Kaplan, 1971). For the ill child (and often his siblings), however, effective coping is contingent upon reduction of anxiety about the illness (Morrissey, 1965). This is best accomplished, according to the protective view, by shielding the child from knowledge of the illness—thus withholding information and diligently maintaining a "normal" family life (Toch, 1964; Howell, 1966; Evans, 1968; Sigler, 1970). As Toch writes:

> The happiest survivals that I have seen were in children where the family was able to treat them just as if nothing had happened, where the parents made their adjustment to their child's disease, tucked it away in the back of their minds, and then went on living (p. 421).

Some professionals have challenged this protective view (Vernick & Karon, 1965; Yudkin, 1967; Kliman, 1968; Martin, 1968; Binger et al., 1969; Easson, 1970; Feinberg, 1970; Kaplan, 1971; Kubler-Ross, 1971; Waechter, 1971). They argue that the greatest source of the child's anxiety is the sense of isolation which he experiences when communication is "managed" to shield him from his illness. Thus, the critical issue is not how successfully parents withhold information or maintain family life as usual, but rather how successfully they provide an environment in which the child feels that the illness is not "too awful to talk about" and that others are willing to support and acknowledge his serious concerns (Vernick & Karon, 1965; Binger et al., 1969; Waechter, 1971). Accord-ing to this view, an open environment[2] facilitates effective coping for children as well as parents and thus should be encouraged as an integral part of the total family experience in coping with the illness and its many consequences (Vernick & Karon, 1965; Kaplan, 1971).

The remainder of this paper is devoted to an examination of family communication about the crisis from the above two perspectives. Parent coping and communication will be discussed first, followed by communication with the ill child and well siblings. The rationale for the protective and open approaches will be discussed in terms of the source of the child's anxiety, his conception of death, and his observed behavioral response to the illness.

PARENT COPING AND COMMUNICATION

The pioneer work of Lindemann on bereavement (1944) and a number of subsequent studies on parents of leukemic children (Bozeman, et al., 1955; Richmond & Waisman, 1955; Natterson & Knudson, 1960; Friedman, et al., 1963; Hamovitch, 1964; Lowenberg,

---

[2] In terms of parent-child communication, it should be emphasized that the concept of "open approach" as discussed throughout the article is *not* equated with informing the child that he is going to die. Rather, it refers to a readiness or willingness to listen and respond to the child's fears and concerns. A statement of Elisabeth Kubler-Ross (1971) illustrates this view: "Never *tell* the patient he is dying . . . When he is ready, and if he has one single person who can listen, he will tell you in his own way (p. 35)."

1970; Wiener, 1970; Hoffman & Futterman, 1971; Kaplan, 1971) have identified the various phases of the crisis and the specific coping tasks which the parents must accomplish—thus, a beginning phase involving the constellation of shock, anger, guilt, and grief, with denial as the prominent defense; a middle phase involving attempts at intellectual mastery followed by concern with the day-to-day management of the child's physical care; and an ending phase involving an emotional acceptance of the disease and resumption of grief work or anticipatory mourning. The importance of accomplishing this grief work—which entails breaking the bondages with the fatally ill or deceased and readjusting to the environment (Lindemann, 1944)—is suggested in each of the studies cited. Thus, Friedman, et al. (1963), note that parents who strongly maintain denial throughout the illness must experience the grief "all at once" at the time of death. For them, death often brings an intense grief reaction in the weeks, months, and sometimes years that follow.

Lindemann (1944) notes that accomplishing the necessary grief work requires a willingness to experience the intense pain of grief and to express the accompanying emotion. Both these processes may be significantly affected by the way in which the parents communicate with each other during the course of the illness (Verwoerdt, 1966; Wiener, 1970; Kaplan, 1971). Thus, Verwoerdt (1966) states:

> (In order to promote the anticipatory grief process) the physician should encourage the parents to give expression to their feelings of grief. The release of emotions will prepare them for the loss and help them resume responsibility to family with greater composure and stabilize and enhance the quality of the last acts of being together with the child (p. 136-7).

Kaplan (1971), in a prospective study of coping patterns in fifty leukemic families describes effective coping, in which open communication is evident, and discrepant coping, in which communication between parents is restricted. Kaplan suggests that when channels of communication remain open between the parents, feelings of grief, concern, fears, etc.—when ready for expression—may be shared openly with the spouse. Encouragement, or at least a lack of discouragement, for moving through the grief process is communicated implicitly by the partner's willingness to provide support and consolation and by his or her own willingness to experience and openly express painful emotions. This mutual willingness to share thoughts and feelings provides a significant source of support in dealing with the emotional and practical demands of the crisis. Restricted communication, however, has the opposite consequences. Often resulting from discrepancies in parents' coping styles (one maintains denial while the other does not), restricted communication may take the following form:

> Open expression of fear, crying, and depression by one parent is perceived (by the other) as a confirmation of one's worst fears . . . that facing the illness will lead to disaster, e.g., to mental breakdown or suicide. Emotion in the spouse is perceived as "weakness", requiring the partner to inhibit expression of feeling in himself because "someone has to be strong". The "strong" spouse who suppresses his own fears and grief is the one to be concerned about, not only for his sake, but for the rest of the family, whose coping he jeopardizes (p. 12).

This prohibition on expression of grief, then, compromises the ability of the family members to resolve important coping tasks and may have more long-term detrimental consequences for the marital relationship. Thus, Kaplan suggests that a legitimate expectation of family members under the stress of coping with a catastrophic illness is having one's needs met for emotional and/or practical support. When one partner fails to respond reciprocally to the legitimate expectations of the other, resentment and dissatisfaction with the spouse's support level inevitably follow, leading to a weakening in the marital relationship itself. When this happens, both parents must not only experience the stress of coping with the illness, but must do so essentially in isolation, with the further burden of a weakened marital relationship precisely at the time when it most needs strengthening. Thus, Verwoerdt (1966) concludes:

> During the time of such a crisis, effective communication between husband and wife is particularly essential. A great deal of support is needed by each spouse, one from the other . . . the stability of the entire family unit depends upon the strength of the parental relationship (p. 135).

COMMUNICATION WITH THE LEUKEMIC CHILD AND SIBLINGS: THE PROTECTIVE APPROACH

In contrast to the approach taken with the parents, the protective view suggests that the ill child's (and often his siblings') emotional well-being is dependent upon shielding him from the meaning of his illness and maintaining a "normal" family life. Thus, Emma Plank (1964), child therapist, writes:

> Life but not death is children's business. When a child who may conceivably die during hospitalization brings up the question of the possibility of his own death, we reassure him with great conviction and help him to deny the possibility (p. 638).

Howell (1966) states:

> One of the ways that this (helping the family to control emotions) can be done is by challenging the family to protect their child from the knowledge that his life span is limited. There is no need for a child to bear the burden of knowingly facing death; the parents can save him this (p. 3).

Toch (1964) more emphatically states:

> I promise the parents that as far as the physicians, nurses, and all the other people who are going to deal with their child are concerned, the child will be surrounded by as normal activity as possible. Nobody is going to regard the child with a long face, but everybody is going to be cheerful and give their child as much of an uplift as if he did not have cancer . . . (p. 421).

In explaining how protection of the child is to be accomplished, Evans (1968) comments:

> The older child requires a detailed explanation. Anemia and "tired blood" concepts of leukemia (to explain why) the child is tired and pale. The cause of this type of anemia is not known. Ways of treating the disease are known and the child will be well again (p. 139).

Siblings are to be given a similar explanation (Evans, 1968). When difficulties with the siblings arise, intensified efforts on the part of the parents to reestablish customary interactions is recommended. As Howell (1966) notes:

Siblings, not knowledgeable as to the severity of the illness will quickly become resentful of the ill child, his demands on the parents, and the attention of family and strangers . . . Thus, suggestions (to maintain consistency and regularity of family life) may have to be reiterated, reworded, and reconfirmed from time to time (throughout the illness) . . . (p. 5).

Rationale: the Source of Anxiety

In one sense, the protective approach to the ill child and siblings discussed above can be seen as a reflection of the general cultural taboo on death (e.g., Feifel, 1963; Kalish, 1969; Kubler-Ross, 1969). More specifically, however, it seems to reflect a concern with the inability of the child's defensive system to cope with the tremendous anxiety which awareness of possible impending death would entail. Thus, Evans (1968) states, in discussing her reasons for restricting illness-related communication with the child:

One often deals with fears (about death) by suppression or rejection and this can be very effective. By open discussion, this excellent defense mechanism is destroyed (p. 138).

In addition to unmanageable anxiety, the child's conception of death and his behavioral response to the illness are also cited as reasons for using a protective approach.

Rationale: The Child's Conception of Death

Only a few studies have been conducted on a child's conception of death (Anthony, 1940; Nagy, 1948; Safier, 1964; Gartley & Bernasconi, 1967); all have been done with healthy children in non-death related circumstances. In general, these studies indicate that a child's conception of death matures developmentally, paralleling the early psychosocial stages of development. Thus, children below five usually view death as reversible—a departure or separation. Children from about six to nine or ten conceptualize death as an inevitable, external process which most often results from the actions of other individuals or purposive forces (e.g., God) and serves as punishment for evil thoughts or deeds. Children above the age of ten begin to view death as an internal process, inherent and universal to all forms of life, including the self.

Studies based on clinical impressions, observations, and staff reports of hospitalized fatally ill children (Natterson & Knudson, 1960; Morrissey, 1965) have largely corroborated the above view, noting a developmental progression of separation, mutilation, and death anxiety. Hamovitch (1964), in a study evaluating the parent participation program at the City of Hope, found the program to be most effective for the youngest children, alleviating much of their separation anxiety, while it was least effective for the adolescents, who displayed anxiety, withdrawal, and depression which deepened with each death of another child on the ward. The latency children, on the other hand, seemed to experience the least anxiety of the three age groups. Hamovitch suggests that they responded mostly along the "pleasure-pain principle" regarding medical procedures, but were too old to experience intense separation anxiety and still too young to be completely cognizant of the implications of their illness.

In terms of implications for practice, the findings of these studies suggest that for the ill child or sibling of latency age and younger, anxiety regarding the meaning of the illness need not be a prominent issue to be dealt with openly by the family or physician. This would be so not only because of the child's defenselessness (as discussed previously) but also because, developmentally, the issue is not a prominent one for the child.

Rationale: The Child's Silent Response

Further evidence for the above conclusion is based on the behavioral response of the hospitalized fatally ill child. This response, in a majority of cases, involves a tendency toward passive silence in which the children seldom verbally express concern with the possibility of their own death or question the nature of their diagnosis (Richmond & Waisman, 1955; Toch, 1964; Agranoff & Mauer, 1965; Yudkin, 1967; Evans, 1968). Richmond & Waisman (1955) note that even adolescents evidence this response, which, according to the authors, may be due to attempts at repression of the anxiety. Thus, even if the latency or younger child has a greater conceptual understanding of death than is currently indicated, the fact that he does not "show interest" (e.g., ask questions about the illness) suggests to proponents of the protective view that he does not want to know about his illness or would find it too threatening to express his concerns openly.

In summary then, the protective view argues that the child's defenses are inadequate for coping with the anxiety that would flow from awareness of possible imminent death. However, if encouraged and strengthened by the adults who care for the child, these defenses can be effective in denying or repressing cues as to the disease prognosis which emanate from the interior of the body and from the altered, emotionally charged environment. Since strengthening the defensive repertoire can lessen anxiety, an open approach to communication in which the child is permitted to discuss his concerns or fears would not be indicated; this would only add new dimensions to the child's existing anxieties regarding separation from parents and painful procedures. Thus, the most therapeutic approach to communication with the fatally ill child and his sibling is likely to be one which "helps the child to firmly deny fears (Plank, 1964)" and which "helps preserve the excellent defenses of suppression and rejection (Evans, 1968)". In practical terms, this therapeutic prescription translates into an optimistic demeanor in communicating with the children (Toch, 1964), with emphasis on getting well (Evans, 1968) and carrying on daily living in as normal a fashion as possible (Toch, 1964; Howell, 1966; Evans, 1968; Sigler, 1970).

Little formal research has been conducted to ascertain the consequences of the protective approach for the adjustment of the individual family members. In terms of the parents, however, it is evident that the approach requires them to engage in opposing coping processes, simultaneously expressing grief-laden emotions to resolve their own loss (Verwoerdt, 1966) and suppressing grief-laden emotions to protect their child (Howell, 1966). Such conflicting expectations are likely to create additional stress for the parents. Proponents of the open environment view suggest that these expectations may also create additional stress for the well siblings and fatally ill child.

COMMUNICATION WITH THE LEUKEMIC CHILD AND SIBLINGS: THE OPEN APPROACH

Opposing the protective approach, proponents of the open view argue that the leukemic child and his siblings need an environment in which they can feel free to ask questions and express concerns, with the knowledge that they will receive honest answers and understanding support from those who care for them (Vernick & Karon, 1965; Binger et al., 1969). This type of environment is necessarily precluded in the protective approach, which requires adults to "manage" all communication so that the child never suspects or discovers his diagnosis or prognosis.

The Source of Anxiety

According to the open view, this process of managing communication is the most detrimental component of the protective approach and the major source of the child's anxiety. Intrinsically involved in the attempt to live life as usual and treat the child as if nothing were happening, it requires avoiding subjects that might lead to the child's questioning of the illness, ignoring some of the child's overt or covert clues regarding his serious concerns, or denying the child's expressed concerns by brushing them aside or giving false reassurance. Sometimes it requires physically distancing oneself from the child to avoid difficult encounters. Glaser and Strauss (1965), in a sociological study of medical personnel's management of communication with the fatally ill adult in a "closed awareness context," illustrate this process. Thus, staff attempt to control the patient's assessment of events and cues which might lead him to suspect his diagnosis. They achieve this control in many ways:

> The physician and nurses may go out of their way to reassure (the patient) that things will turn out "all right" and indeed are "coming along fine" ... If he asks ... "Am I going to die," ... they may change the subject without answering the question, turn it aside with a stock answer (e.g., "We all have to go sometime") ... or simply lie ... They may comment favorably on his daily appearance ... or on his imminent or eventual return home ... Space is also carefully managed so that talk about (the patient) occurs away from his presence ... If a nurse believes her involvement with or sadness about the patient might give the secret away, she may move quickly outside his visual range ... She may even request an assignment away from him ... Sometimes when the patient is extremely close to death ... staff members tend to go no further than the door-way ... (In addition) disclosing cues are minimized most subtly by reducing the range of expression and topic ... hence the conventionally bland or cheerful faces of nurse and physician. (Nurses and physicians) also censor and select conversational topics ... steering conversation away from potentially revealing subjects and towards safer ones (p. 36-37).

Indications that some of the identical processes noted by Glaser and Strauss also occur with the fatally ill child can be seen throughout the literature. Thus, Karon and Vernick (1968), in a study of fifty-one leukemic children at the National Cancer Institute state:

> Staff's early reluctance to discuss leukemia with their patients was due to apprehension over questions about prognosis: would they be obliged to intone a death sentence? Frequently physicians and nurses were so concerned about this that they were afraid to start a conversation on any but the most trivial subjects (p. 274).

Hamovitch (1964) also notes, in conclusion to his evaluation of the parent participation program at the City of Hope:

> Staff and parents were most uncomfortable with (older) children ... there was recognition of the child's awareness, yet an inability to deal with it satisfactorily. This generally was handled by an avoidance of "dangerous" topics and sometimes by physical avoidance also—thereby probably reinforcing the child's anxiety (p. 115).

Binger et al. (1969) state in their study of twenty leukemic families that some parents believed the professional staff became more remote, physically avoiding the children as death approached. In a two-year study of 46 parents of leukemic children, Friedman (1967) notes:

> Parents often are reluctant to acknowledge how their child is feeling, believing that they should constantly cheer him up . . . telling him such things as, "you look great," when he knows this is obviously not true . . . (p. 503).

Yudkin (1967) observes other attempts to avoid dealing with the child's anxieties and concerns, which are especially evident when a death occurs on the ward:

> There is whispering and scuffling behind the screens . . . nurses and doctors are preoccupied and don't answer questions and are unduly irritable . . . above all, there is the stupid pretence that nothing at all unusual is happening (p. 40).

Explanations to other children of the death, if given, usually amount to statements that the dead child is in another hospital or has gone home (Natterson & Knudson, 1960; Vernick & Karon, 1965).

The open view argues that although such communication processes as those described above are implemented to protect the child, they instead foster a pervasive sense of isolation, increasing the child's existing anxieties and promoting new areas of concern. Thus, in addition to coping with anxieties about the illness itself, the child must cope with the fact that the adults in his environment can no longer be relied upon to deal with him in a trustworthy and honest fashion. As Martin (1968) suggests in his study of thirty fatally and non-fatally ill children undergoing surgery:

> The obvious paradox in verbally stating that there is nothing to worry about while non-verbally denying this statement with anxious facial expressions or body gestures not only undermines the child's confidence in the communicator but may also undermine his confidence in his own vulnerability . . . When this type of paradoxical and evasive communication is given to the child by significant adults in his environment, all communication soon becomes suspect in the eyes of the child (p. 41, 71).

The end result then is that the child feels lonely and abandoned at the very time when he is most in need of meaningful communication with a trustworthy adult (Vernick & Karon, 1965; Binger et al., 1969). Thus, he derives his own distorted conclusions about the cause of his physical condition, begins to distrust the thought that others are genuinely concerned with his welfare, and feels increasingly threatened by his seeming inability to make sense out of the many conflicting messages given to him by his environment.

Similar consequences are noted for the well siblings who observe the lack of "normal" family life but are not included in the family problem. Thus, they often perceive the attention given to the leukemic child as indicating the parents' rejection of themselves and are left alone to deal with the thought that they too will become seriously ill or die (Binger et al., 1969; McCollum & Schwartz, 1972). Coping with these by-products of the protective approach, argues the open view, is the ill child's and siblings' most difficult psychological task.

The Child's Conception of Death

While the open and protective views differ in explaining the major source of the child's anxieties, they also differ in explaining the role of the child's immature conception of death. Thus, the open view argues that instead of alleviating anxiety, the child's immature conceptions lead to feelings of guilt and personal responsibility for the illness. Beverly, (1936) notes that, in response to the question, "Why do children become sick?", ninety percent of a group of children with diabetes and heart disease responded, "Because they are bad". Schowalter (1970), suggests:

> For the child with a serious or fatal illness, guilt is often almost as common as fear . . . He may understand his regressive illness as deserved punishment for real or imagined wrong doing. As if to confirm his punishment fantasy, hospitalization takes him from his parents, and he is subjected to numerous painful tests and therapies. Instead of being expiated by these inflictions, he finds himself worsening. At this point many young patients seem to give up and resign themselves to whatever may come (p. 56).

Such feelings of responsibility may be equally severe for the siblings, who often perceive the anger and resentment they expressed during the child's remission as the cause of subsequent exacerbations (Binger, et al., 1969; McCollum and Schwartz, 1972). Depressive symptoms, nightmares, aggressive reactive behavior, school problems, etc. are frequently the result (Binger, et al., 1969).

Yudkin (1967) also suggests that the child's guilt feelings may be intensified by the parents' changed behavior, since the child concludes that the change is due to something terrible which he has done. Yudkin considers such phenomena important reasons for giving the dying child an opportunity to express his fears and fantasies.

> We may find it relatively easy to reassure a child about terrifying visons, about loneliness and fear, about punishment for supposed misdeeds and about his anxiety over his parents' obvious concern. The fears about the fantasies may be more real and more urgent than any fear about the approach of death itself (p. 39).

Using a protective approach, however, the "fears about the fantasies" remain the central conceptual perspective from which the child interprets the behavior of those in his environment. Consequently, anxiety is increased and guilt is added to fear.

The Silent Response

If the child has a good deal of fear and disturbing fantasies why does he respond to his illness in a passive, unquestioning manner? Proponents of the open view offer several reasons, all of which assume that the child is aware of the seriousness of his illness but that adults in his environment are unable to acknowledge or deal with this awareness. Thus Vernick and Karon (1965) state:

> When the physician gives the fateful news to the parents, the child immediately "knows" that he has something very serious because his entire environment changes. His parents, no matter how hard they try, cannot conceal their own grave concern. The child quickly senses that the people whom he had come to trust and love are now keeping something from him, something frightening (p. 395).

The notion that denial and repression can successfully prevent such awareness may have more to do with the adult's own denial and wishful thinking than with the child's dynamics. As Yudkin (1967) notes:

> We are often unaware that the child is frightened of dying, either because it is inconceivable or because we will not allow ourselves to think about it (p. 39).

Thus, in terms of the silent response, younger leukemic children may be utilizing the symbolic language of play, painting, and drawing to communicate their awareness (Morrissey, 1965; Kubler-Ross, 1971), with the adult ignoring these subtle cues and interpreting the lack of direct questioning as unawareness (Solnit & Green, 1963). Older children may be silent in an attempt to "protect" the adult (Morrissey, 1965; Yudkin, 1967; Binger et al., 1969; Schowalter, 1970). Thus, Binger et al. state:

> As parents attempt to protect their children from the concerns of the illness, older leukemic children attempt similarly to protect their parents. The children who were perhaps the loneliest of all were those who were aware of their diagnosis but at the same time recognized that their parents did not wish them to know. As a result there was little or no meaningful communication (p. 415).

The most important reason for the child's silent response, however, is this very wish not to have the child know—which, in essence, "prohibits" the child from responding in an open, questioning way. Thus, Schowalter (1970) comments:

> (Fatally ill children) seldom talk of their impending death. Because of intellectual immaturity or emotional defenses, some children are not aware that they are dying. A greater number, however, don't talk about their death because those around them overtly or covertly forbid it (p. 51-52).

Morrissey (1965), in his study of death anxiety in fifty fatally ill children, concludes:

> The children emphatically perceive parental anxiety and embarrassment regarding death . . . and would endure the "role playing" of their parents and staff . . . an experience characterized by a stoic kind of "make the best of it but let's not talk about it" atmosphere . . . (p. 333).

Friedman et al. (1963) indicate the extent to which adults might prohibit communication when noting that most parents in their study "attempted to shield their children from ever hearing the word leukemia" (p. 615). Several studies suggest that siblings may experience the same prohibition (with similar results) after the actual death of the child or other family member (Cain, Fast, & Erickson, 1964; Becker & Margolin, 1967; Kliman, 1968). Thus, Becker and Margolin describe the reaction of one family in their study:

> The children would visit the cemetery with their father, place flowers on the grave and be witness to relatives crying without anyone mentioning their mother's death or burial. During these visits, the children never asked why they were there. This suggests to us that the father's silence communicated to them a feeling of the taboo nature of the subject (p. 755).

The fatally ill child (and his siblings), then, sense the adult's unwillingness to deal with the problem openly. The child fears, speculates Waechter (1971), that if he expresses his questions and concerns openly, adults will reject him. In an effort to avoid loss of contact and maintain approval of significant adults, he quickly learns to keep his thoughts to himself (Karon & Vernick, 1968).

Awareness Discrepancy

The interplay between the adult's denial and prohibition on illness-related communication and the child's unquestioning response may be described in terms of a "vicious cycle" which leads to an increasing discrepancy between the child's experience of his illness and the adult's perception of that experience. Thus, as discussed above, the child senses the adult's unwillingness or inability to talk with him and so refrains from communicating his anxieties, fears, and concerns directly to the adult. The fact that the child says or asks little is then cited by the adult as "evidence" that he is either not aware of the seriousness of his situation or that he is effectively utilizing mechanisms of denial and repression. This interpretation of the child's behavior, in turn, provides further support for the adult's own denial of the child's anxiety and leads the adult to fortify his on-going efforts to "protect" the child through prohibiting any communication that may allude to the implications of the illness. The adult, as a result of lack of meaningful communication with his child, becomes increasingly unable to accurately perceive, assess, and respond to the child's inner experience. The child, in turn, responds to the adult's apparent "unawareness" with further withdrawal, accompanied by feelings of loneliness and increased anxiety.

This discrepancy between the child's experience and the adult's belief about that experience has been documented in the one study to date which has employed psychological tests as opposed to behavioral observations as its major research instrument. Eugenia Waechter (1971) conducted a study of sixty-four hospitalized children, sixteen of whom were fatally ill, utilizing projective tests and interviews with parents. All of the children were between the ages of six and ten—the age group which was observed in previous studies (Hamovitch, 1964; Natterson & Knudson, 1960; and Morrissey, 1965) to experience anxiety related primarily to medical procedures rather than separation or death, and to have fewer adjustment problems than children in the younger or older age groups. In Waechter's study, the sixteen fatally ill children evidenced twice as much generalized anxiety as their non-fatally ill counterparts and related stories concerning loneliness, separation, and death much more frequently than did the comparison non-fatally ill children—they had never discussed such feelings directly with either staff or parents. In comparing the parent interviews with children's test responses, the awareness discrepancy was striking. Thus, parents would often state that their children either had no awareness of the seriousness of the illness or that they thought they had "tired blood" or "anemia". The children would subsequently respond to the projective tests stating, among other things, that the story figures had "leukemia," or "cancer," "died and was buried with a big shovel," or "went to heaven but didn't like it—because God wasn't there" (p. 1170, 1172). Waechter concludes:

> (These findings) suggest that knowledge is communicated to the child by the change in affect which he encounters in his total environment after the diagnosis is made and by his perceptiveness of other nonverbal cues. (They) also imply a deepening of isolation when the child becomes aware of the evasiveness which meets expression of his concern (p. 1170).

THE OPEN APPROACH:
CONCLUSIONS, PRESCRIPTIONS, EVIDENCE FROM RESEARCH

Perhaps the most serious concern for proponents of the open approach, then, is suggested in the findings of Waechter's research: the fatally ill child experiences a great deal of anxiety relating to separation, loneliness, and death, but adults in the child's environment are unaware and/or unable to deal with this anxiety. Remedying this state of affairs has become a major effort of the open view proponents. Thus, Waechter states:

The question of whether a child should be told that his illness is fatal is meaningless. Rather the questions and concerns that are conscious for the child threatened with death should be dealt with in such a way that the child does not feel further isolated and alienated from his parents and other meaningful adults. There should be no curtain of silence around his most intense fears . . . (p. 1172).

Proponents of the open view suggest that conveying to the child a willingness to deal with his concerns may be accomplished in a variety of ways—from taking initative in preparing the child for hospitalizations, clinic visits, procedures, etc. (Kliman, 1968; Easson, 1970), to discussing with the child the concerns and questions which he does verbally express (Vernick & Karon, 1965; Binger, et al., 1969; Schowalter, 1970; Waechter, 1971), to anticipating and expressing for the child those concerns which he indicates behaviorally but cannot express verbally (Vernick & Karon, 1965; Yudkin, 1967; Kliman, 1968). The child's questions regarding the implications of his illness may be dealt with by acknowledging that the illness is serious and that some children do die from a serious illness, but then reinforcing and reaffirming hope for the child by specifying the diligent efforts of the medical staff and the reasons for treatment procedures (Vernick & Karon, 1965). Fear of questions regarding the prognosis should not determine the approach to take in communicating with the child; rather, apprehension regarding these questions should be subordinated to the larger, more important task of becoming aware of and available to the child and his life and death concerns . . .

Evidence from the literature as to the outcome of this open approach is relatively sparse. Binger et al. (1969) report two children (both adolescents) in their study were told they had leukemia for which there was no known cure. They state:

There was no evidence during the course of the illness or in interviews with the families after death that these children had greater difficulty coping than their counterparts to whom nothing had been said directly. Both these families reported a more meaningful relationship with the child than they had ever experienced before. They thought this change was due largely to the frank discussion of the diagnosis and the open communication within the families (p. 115).

More formal research evidence is found in Waechter's study (1971). Only two of the sixteen fatally ill children were given an opportunity to discuss their concerns with their parents. Both these children had cystic fibrosis, a chronic, handicapping but eventually fatal disease. Waechter found a highly significant relationship between the opportunity to discuss and the child's overall test scores. She states this supports the prediction that:

giving a child such an opportunity does not heighten death anxiety; on the contrary, understanding acceptance and conveyance of permission to discuss any aspect of the illness may decrease feelings of isolation and alienation and the sense that his illness is too terrible to discuss (p. 1170).

Other, more subjective evidence comes from a two-year program at the National Cancer Institute (Vernick & Karon, 1965; Karon & Vernick, 1968). The program included fifty-one children from the ages of nine to twenty, hospitalized for leukemia. Utilizing life space interviews with the children and weekly group meetings with children, parents, and staff, the goal of the program was to "develop an environment in which (children) feel perfectly safe to ask any question and completely confident of receiving an honest answer" (1965, p. 393). Every child was told his diagnosis but at the same time was given an outline for a potentially helpful therapeutic regime. On the basis of observations and discussions with these children, the authors conclude that there were no significant adjustment problems in any of the fifty-one patients. Withdrawal and depression noted by other researchers (Richmond & Waisman, 1955; Natterson & Knudson, 1960) occurred infrequently and were always transient. In their discussion of the program, the authors note:

> One of every child's most frequently expressed desires was the wish to have his physician discuss everything that pertained to his treatment with him . . . Maintaining good communication was so central to these children's sense of well-being that any evasiveness on the part of the physician . . . provoked hostility (1968, p. 275-276).

The authors also state (1968) that when the children were given the opportunity, they asked many technical and highly searching questions about their illness and its implications. This indicated not only the children's intense concerns but also their need to make sense out of the things that were happening to them—to justify such events as painful procedures and place them in an overall context of attempts to get them well.

The authors conclude (1965) that parents and staff—who have more emotional strength than the children—must be the ones to take initiative in talking about death, since the children will be unlikely to do this on their own.

> Contrary to reports that they seem to react with "an air of passive acceptance and resignation (Richmond & Waisman, 1955)" experience with our group indicates that every child who is lying in bed gravely ill is worrying about dying and is eager to have someone help him talk about it. If he is passive, it may be only a reflection of how freely the environment encourages him to express his concerns (1965, p. 395).

REFERENCES

Agranoff, J. H., & Mauer, A.M. What should the child with leukemia be told? *American Journal of Diseases of Children*, 1965, 110, 231.

Anthony, S. *The child's discovery of death*. New York: Harcourt, Brace, 1940.

Becker, D., & Margolin, F. How surviving parents handled their young children's adaptation to the crisis of loss. *American Journal of Orthopsychiatry*, 1967, 37, 753-757.

Beverly, B.I. The effect of illness upon emotional development. *Journal of Pediatrics*, 1936, 8, 533.

Binger, C.M., Ablin, A.R., Feurstein, R.C., Kushner, J.H., Zoger, S., & Mikkelsen, C. Childhood leukemia: Emotional impact on patient and family. *New England Journal of Medicine*, 1969, 280, 414-418.

Bozeman, M.F., Orbach, C.E., & Sutherland, A.M. Psychological impact of cancer and its treatment. III. The adaptation of mothers to the threatened loss of their children through leukemia: Parts I & II. *Cancer*, 1955, 8, 1-33.

Cain, A.C., Fast, I., & Erickson, M.E. Children's disturbed reactions to the death of a sibling. *American Journal of Orthopsychiatry*, 1964, 34, 741-52.

Easson, W.M. *The dying child*. Springfield: Charles C. Thomas, 1970.

Evans, A.E. If a child must die. *New England Journal of Medicine*, 1968, 278, 138-142.

Feifel, H. Death. In N.L. Farberow (Ed.), *Taboo Topics*. New York: Atherton Press, 1963.

Feinberg, D. Preventive therapy with siblings of a dying child. *American Academy of Child Psychiatry*, 1970, 9, 644-667.

Friedman, S.B. Care of the family of the child with cancer. *Pediatrics*, 1967, 40, 498-503.

Friedman, S.B., Chodoff, P., Mason, J.W., & Hamburg, D.A. Behavioral observations on parents anticipating the death of a child. *Pediatrics*, 1963, 32, 610-625.

Gartley, W., & Bernasconi, M. The concept of death in children. *Journal of Genetic Psychology*, 1967, 110, 71-85.

Glaser, B.G., & Strauss, A.L. *Awareness of dying*. Chicago: Aldine Press, 1965.

Hamovitch, M.B. *The parent and the fatally ill child*. Duarte: City of Hope Medical Center, 1964.

Hoffman, I., & Futterman, E.H. Coping with waiting: Psychiatric intervention and study in the waiting room of a pediatric oncology clinic. *Comprehensive Psychiatry*, 1971, 12, 67-81.

Howell, D. A child dies. *Journal of Pediatric Surgery*, 1966, 1, 2-7.

Kalish, R.A. The effects of death upon the family. In L. Pearson (Ed.), *Death and dying*. Cleveland: The Press of Case Western Reserve University, 1969.

Kaplan, D.M. Coping with childhood leukemia: A severe family crisis, Part I. Unpublished paper, Stanford University School of Medicine, 1971, 1-18.

Karon, M., & Vernick, J. An approach to the emotional support of fatally ill children. *Clinical Pediatrics*, 1968, 7, 274-280.

Kliman, G. *Psychological emergencies of childhood*. New York: Grune & Stratton, 1968.

Kubler-Ross, E. *On death and dying*. New York: The Macmillan Company, 1969.

————. Quoted in Dealing with death. *Medical World News*, (May 21) 1971, 12, 30-36.

Leukemia: Where medicine stands today. *Medical World News* (April 2) 1971, 12, 34-37.

Lindemann, E. Symptomatology and management of acute grief. *American Journal of Psychiatry*, 1944, 101, 141-148.

Lowenberg, J.S. The coping behaviors of fatally ill adolescents and their parents. *Nursing Forum*, 1970, 9, 269-287.

Lyman, M.S., & Burchenal, J.H. Acute leukemia. *The American Journal of Nursing*, 1963, 63, 82-86.

Martin, R.L. *The acute situational crisis and communication theory*. Unpublished Doctoral Dissertation, School of Social Work, University of Southern California, 1968.

McCollum, A.T., & Schwartz, A.H. Social Work and the Mourning Parent. *Social Work*, 1972, 17, 25-36.

Morrissey, J.R. Death anxiety in children with a fatal illness. In H.J. Parad (Ed.), *Crisis intervention: Selected readings*. New York: Family Service Association of America, 1965.

Nagy, M.H. The child's theories concerning death. *Journal of Genetic Psychology*, 1948, 73, 3-27.

Natterson, J.M., & Knudson, A.G. Observations concerning fear of death in fatally ill children and their mothers. *Psychosomatic Medicine*, 1960, 22, 456-465.

Plank, E. Death on a children's ward. *Medical Times*, 1964, 92, 638-644.

Richmond, J.B. & Waisman, H.A. Psychologic aspects of management of children with malignant diseases. *American Journal of Diseases of Children*, 1955, 89, 42-47.

Safier, G.A. A study in relationships between the life and death concepts in children. *Journal of Genetic Psychology*, 1964, 105, 283-294.

Schowalter, J.E. The child's reaction to his own terminal illness. In B. Schoenberg, A.C. Carr, D. Peretz, & A.H. Kutscher (Eds.), *Loss and grief: Psychological management in medical practice*. New York: Columbia University Press, 1970.

Sigler, A. The leukemic child and his family: An emotional challenge. In M. Debuskey (Ed.), *The chronically ill child and his family*. Springfield: Charles C. Thomas, 1970.

Solnit, A.J., & Green, M. The pediatric management of the dying child: Part II. The child's reaction to the fear of dying. In A.J. Solnit & S.A. Provence (Eds.), *Modern perspectives in child development*. New York: International Universities Press, 1963.

Toch, R. Management of the child with a fatal disease. *Clinical Pediatrics*, 1964, 3, 418-427.

Vernick, J., & Karon, M. Who's afraid of death on a leukemia ward? *American Journal of Diseases of Children*, 1965, 109, 393-397.

Verwoerdt, A. *Communication with the fatally ill*. Springfield: Charles C. Thomas, 1966.

Waechter, E. H. Children's awareness of fatal illness. *American Journal of Nursing*, 1971, 71, 1168-1172.

Wiener, J.M. Reaction of the family to the fatal illness of a child. In B. Schoenberg, A.C. Carr, D. Peretz, & A.H. Kutscher (Eds.), *Loss and grief: Psychological management in medical practice*. New York: Columbia University Press, 1970.

Yudkin, S. Children and death. *The Lancet*, 1967, 1, 37-41.

CHAPTER
5

Story of a First-Born*

Wende Kernan Bowie

In the last two decades, popular informative literature and the burgeoning availability of natural childbirth training classes have almost erased the image of fear and pain that most of our mothers associated with childbirth, creating in its place a much more fearless, hopeful outlook on the process of birth and fetal development. The practice of obstetrics, pre-natal and neonatal care has improved, brushing away much of the mystery and uncertainty of the past. The voluminous literature written for expectant parents is overwhelmingly optimistic; there are statistics and more statistics to show the decreasing incidence of birth defects and fetal or neonatal deaths.

But despite the impression an expectant mother gets, mishaps to mother and infant during pregnancy and birth continue to occur. The percentages are decreasing, but the actual number is still quite large. In 1974 in the United States, it is estimated that 660 mothers died as a result of complications of pregnancy, childbirth and the puerperium. It is estimated that each year over 200,000 infants have defects that are evident at birth or during the first few years of life. Almost 20 per cent of the newborns or more than 600,000 infants per year require care for some form of illness during the newborn period.[1]

---

* All the names mentioned in this article are fictitious, except for my own, my husband's and my son's.
[1] Statistics are estimates given by the National Foundation March of Dimes.

45

What happens to the mother and infant when there is trouble? What normal emotional changes can she expect to have if her child is either ill at birth or needs intensive care for a few days after its birth? How can she best deal with the situation if she must leave her infant in the hospital? What resources are available to her both inside the hospital and at home? What role can her husband take, and what is the status of the pediatrician should the infant be hospitalized in an intensive care unit? These and many other questions can and should be answered within the popular literature, not to frighten, but to inform and prepare expectant parents, so that they do not become mere victims, but active, knowledgeable participants in the process of curing and nurturing their seriously or not so seriously ill infant.

Michael

My husband and I shared our culture's optimism toward childbirth as we approached the coming of our first child last spring. My pregnancy had been a happy one. I was healthy, and I worked until two weeks before Michael was born. My husband and I began Lamaze training, and toward the end of March, I went into labor and was admitted to our community's excellent teaching hospital, where our child was to be delivered. The story of how we two — prospective parents totally unprepared for anything to go wrong — dealt with what happened follows.

MONDAY MARCH 24th

As my husband left my women's hospital room that bright afternoon, I said to him, "Lee, we have a son! We have a son!" I was happy; I was exhausted; and I couldn't possibly sleep; I wanted to call just one more person to tell them our child was finally born! I wanted to tell the world.

That was the last happy moment I was to have for a long time, and as I write this now, I look back on it as Camelot. My newborn baby weighed in at a healthy 7 lbs. 2 oz., and I felt joyful and awed when they placed him in my arms and wheeled us in our triumphant journey out of the delivery room.

That evening an intern came to my room to tell me that there was trouble with my child; he had been born with a high percentage of red blood cells; they had drained some blood from his body and had replaced it with plasma to thin it out so that his heart would not have to work so hard to pump thick blood. The intern informed me that without this exchange transfusion, Michael would have died within hours of a cerebral hemorrhage, but that he thought they had probably transfused him in time. I was also told that Michael was still "downstairs" under observation in a special nursery, but that he would be brought up to the regular nursery on my floor by midnight or so.

I was dismayed. I called Lee who came right over. We talked the whole thing over with the intern again. "Was there any brain damage?" we asked.

Luckily, the answer was no. Midnight did not seem very far away, and I needed some sleep before then, so Lee went back to a friend's house, and I lay back, trying unsuccessfully to rest.

But my episiotomy started to hurt. I was exhausted. I felt like a victim, and I didn't really know how my baby was. Midnight came and went and I fabricated reasons why the nurses had not brought Michael to my room. Perhaps they were planning to bring him to me for the 4 a.m. feeding. I tried to protect myself during those early morning hours from realizing that something was seriously wrong.

TUESDAY MARCH 25th

I slept only an hour or two all night. I was very worried and upset by this time, almost to the point of panic. I had waited all night for the nurses to bring Michael to my room; no one had told me why he was not with me. A group of doctors came to see me. I could hear them reviewing my case outside my room in low voices. It made me angry. I thought they were concealing facts from me. "Why didn't someone tell me about my baby?", I thought.

Finally, the doctors stood at the foot of my bed. One of them told me that my blood pressure was too high. I said, "Of course my blood pressure is too high, I'm worried about my baby!" Honestly, I was thinking, what happens to me is so very unimportant; of course I have high blood pressure! I've not slept a wink for waiting all night and worrying and hoping. The doctor replied curtly that he certainly knew more about my condition than I did and asked me to bare my knee so that he could check my reflexes. My reflexes were fine. The doctor turned on his heel and without another word to me, left the room, followed by the others. I was once again left alone with my thoughts, which were becoming progressively more ominous. There was not a word about Michael.

If it hadn't been for Lee, I couldn't have dealt adequately with this day. Later, after he arrived, we were told Michael was to be kept "downstairs" "a while longer." They suspected there was something wrong with his heart. The news was getting worse and worse. We were both horribly anxious. No one had any definite answers. Had my head been clear at the time, I would have realized that there was one set of doctors dealing with my physical self and another set of doctors dealing with Michael's physical self. None of them were very aware or sensitive in dealing with the emotional stress on me which was, due to the separation between me and my infant, becoming progressively more serious.

Where in heavens name *was* "downstairs" anyway?

At about this point in our thoughts, a student nurse came into the room with some pills for me. When I asked what they were, she replied that they were valium and phenobarbital and that they would "really knock me out." I didn't want to take them, because I wanted to have a clear head to understand what the doctors had to say about Michael. I wanted to see him! The only way to find out what these pills were for was to call the doctor, so Lee did. It took Lee two insistent requests to get past the nurse at his office. The nurse did not know why I had to take the pills; she simply said that I must take them. Finally the doctor came on the line and the following conversation ensued: "Mr. Bowie, I prescribed those pills for your wife; do you know what will happen if she doesn't take them?" In kind, Lee responded, "No, but I think it would be nice if somebody told us." And finally, the doctor said, "There's a good chance she may have convulsions." Of course that settled it. I took the tranquilizers, but it certainly took a lot of panache on Lee's part to find out why they were necessary. Of course I was not allowed to walk, as I was not trusted to keep my balance under such heavy medication.

So, drugged, and in a wheelchair, I was taken to see my baby for the very first time. I was not prepared for this by anything I had read, heard, or learned during my pregnancy, and I had acquired a considerable amount of knowledge about birth, babies and hospitals through Lamaze training, a baby-care course, and much reading of the literature. Most of all, I did not know what I was going to do about nursing my baby if he was to be kept "downstairs." I wanted to nurse him. I had decided long before to breastfeed my baby. At this point, though, I was embarrassed to insist and afraid to ask about it.

The observation nursery was part of the newborn intensive care unit at this hospital. It was a room, neon-lit, with one whole wall of observation windows. It contained a lot of equipment — isolettes, bilirubin lights, scales, examining tables, another scrub sink, oxygen outlets, heart and respiration monitors and, last but not least, babies. Visitors had to wear a sterile gown from neck to mid-calf which tied in the back. We had to scrub with yellow soap from finger-tip to elbow and to remove all rings, watches and jewelry every time we entered the nursery. Eventually I stopped wearing my wedding and engagement rings altogether as I had to remove them to a safe place so often, I was afraid I'd lose them.

Most of the newborn babies spent twelve hours at this nursery being observed for irregularities and then were transferred up to the healthy nursery on the maternity floor. Michael had been here for twenty-four hours. He was pointed out to us. He was being given oxygen in a hood, but it was possible to disconnect the hose from the hood, pick him up, and hold him with the tube pointed directly under his nose. So I sat there in my wheelchair holding my baby for the very first time and holding the oxygen tube to his nose; my husband and the nurse watched Michael and me. Later I was given a bottle of formula to feed him. It took some juggling, but Lee held the oxygen tube and I held Michael and fed him. I wondered if I would be able to nurse Michael when my milk came in, and I did not dare ask why Michael was getting oxygen. I felt privileged just to be allowed to hold him. He was adorable.

When we were finished feeding him, there was nothing left to do there, so Lee took me back to my room. It was then that the flood of maternal feelings overcame me. The sense of separation from Michael was unbearable. I felt a strong need to be near him. It was agony, and I was very frightened that this separation would interfere with my future relationship with this baby for whom I was responsible.

WEDNESDAY MARCH 26th

Michael, we discovered, was a puzzle to all his doctors. He breathed too fast, and the eight specialists who were trying to diagnose his problem were stymied. First they thought it was his heart; but the pediatric cardiologist we spoke to told us it probably was not; then they thought it was his kidneys; but after tests, they discovered it was not. Michael was enigma. I was, I must admit, a bit proud of having given birth to an enigma. To me he was a loveable enigma.

THURSDAY MARCH 27th

Michael, they said, had early signs of a bacterial infection. He would need, they said, to stay in the hospital for at least ten more days. I was not relieved to hear this. How could I stand being separated from him for that long! It seemed like the last straw — I collapsed into tears. He was *my* baby! I wanted him near me!

When I saw him next he had an intravenous needle in his head! They had shaved his hair in an ugly strip in order to find the veins. They had placed a plastic bag over his penis to collect a 24-hour urine sample for diagnostic studies. He was in an isolette, his legs were tied down and his hands also, so he wouldn't push away his tubes and his oxygen mask. I was afraid, so afraid to touch him.

FRIDAY MARCH 28th

At eight in the morning the intern came into my room and told me without ceremony that he thought it was time I went home — that the hospital was no place for me. "It's up to my private obstetrician to tell me when to go home," I replied. After all, I had been on phenobarbital continuously; they had finally stopped giving it to me Thursday night. My blood pressure was still not down to normal. I did not feel reassured at all about my physical condition. And most of all, I did not want to leave my baby there. But I never had a chance to say this last; I sensed that the intern did not want to hear about it, did not consider it a part of his job to discuss this difficult issue with me. The intern, who looked and acted, incidentally, at least ten years my junior, told me that well, "we" are "watching over you" when your doctor isn't here, and that "we" think it is time you left here.

Check-out time at the hospital was 2 p.m. My obstetrician usually came to see me about that time. I told the intern that I was not going anywhere until I got the okay from my obstetrician. My husband was teaching that day, and he could not drive me home until evening. In most cases patients in a hospital are happy to be told to leave, but my case was very different, because leaving the hospital meant leaving my baby. I wished I had been given some advance warning; I knew that I needed time to prepare myself for the wrenching sadness, fear and disappointment of going home with no baby to put into the cheerful nursery Lee and I had prepared.

Somehow I got through that day. I just had to grit my teeth and get through it. I walked down to the nursery one last time to see Michael and wondered what it would be like to be so far away from him. I wondered what it would be like to be at home, alone, recovering from the birth, with no baby to nurse, with my milk coming in. Lee came and helped me pack. We left in the evening.

SATURDAY MARCH 29th

I tried to resume my normal life, but I was still very tired. I had not asked them at the hospital whether I could breastfeed. I took it for granted that I would not be allowed to. They did say that I could express milk and freeze it in two ounce quantities, and that they would then feed it to my baby. But they would not begin doing this until I could produce the 8 ounces per day which was Michael's diet. I was desperately worried that I would not be able to produce that amount, and without Lee's constant encouragement and support I would never have been able to do it. I used a hand pump and my breasts were very sore. It was all I could do to express milk every four hours. I was exhausted from the birth too.

I hoped that Michael would improve and would by some miracle stop breathing too fast. Michael's pediatrician told us that sometimes babies have difficulty at first, but with proper treatment, the rapid breathing diminishes. No one finds out why it happened, but the baby develops normally from then on. My constant thought during all of this uncertainty about Michael's future was that if he should come home I should keep my milk flowing so that I would be able to breastfeed him. It, the breastfeedings, was very important to me; I thought that without it I would be unable to develop a good mother-infant relationship.

I was miserable at home. It was my first baby and I had looked forward to the responsibility of caring for him eagerly, though not without the usual trepidations. My fears about my ability to really love and nurture my baby were greatly magnified because we were apart and because the nursery provided for all Michael's needs. They asked no help from me. I feared that this alienation from my baby would continue into our future relationship. There was one thing that I alone could give Michael: my breast milk. And to this end Lee and I worked to stimulate my breasts to produce.

SUNDAY MARCH 30th

Lee and I went in to see Michael. Dr. Cousins, Michael's pediatrician, was there and several other doctors. Michael was tired. I watched as Dr. Cousins examined him. It was agony to see other people touch Michael. He still seemed a part of myself, but separated, kept in a hospital nursery, where I had "visiting" privileges — I had not even changed his diapers yet, and I had fed him only three or four times. He was almost a week old. I was afraid that if he ever came home he would seem like someone else's child.

I felt very strange with these new feelings — I had never thought before I gave birth that I would experience such intense and disparate emotions. The strength of my love for Michael was almost overwhelming at times, especially when Dr. Cousins examined him that day. I had to leave the room because when Dr. Cousins picked him up and let his head fall back, it came home to me as at no other time that Michael was indeed a very sick baby. I wanted to deny that knowledge as long as I could. I wanted to hold Michael and love him and touch him and care for him and these were all new feelings for me. I was embarrassed to admit them to the nursing staff or the team of doctors because my emotional life was so unfamiliar to me. In this medical context, I wondered what use I could be and where I could fit in.

The medical staff looked at Michael from one perspective — that of diagnosing him. They still didn't know what was wrong. I looked at Michael from another — I was his mother and I wanted desperately to be near him. I hated to see other people touch him.

I finally got the courage to express some of these feelings to Dr. Cousins, and he said that they were the most natural ones in the world. He immediately got the consent of the specialists to allow me to breastfeed Michael in a day or so, as soon as he was off the antibiotics. This was just wonderful! But if I had not had the courage to ask, would anyone have offered to let me breastfeed? If I had not had Dr. Cousins to intercede for me, would I have been deprived of even this?

At this point in the attempts to diagnose Michael's troubles, the doctors thought he had a weak heart. They thought that he either had some viral infection of the muscle or that he had a congenital heart defect. But they didn't know the answers. Dr. Cousins told us that allowing the breastfeeding was extremely unorthodox; in fact, it had probably never been done before. But it was the happiest moment of my life when I was told that I could breastfeed my baby. I wondered if I would have to do it in public the very first time.

MONDAY MARCH 31st

Finally, seven full days after Michael was born, my milk really came in. Perhaps psychologically it had something to do with my new knowledge that I could breastfeed the next day, and I had better be ready so that it would be easy for him! If in fact he had a weak heart, I did not want to exhaust him with the breastfeeding. It takes more energy for a baby to nurse. I could not go to the hospital every three hours and nurse Michael, I was too tired, it was too far to drive, it would adversely affect my milk supply. I therefore had to pump part of the milk and let Michael nurse for only some of the feedings. The milk which was pumped was then frozen and carried into the hospital. The nurses would feed Michael my breast milk by bottle.

We rented a breast pump, electric, from La Leche League for $ .25 a day so that I could express milk. In spite of my determination to provide my baby with milk, I could not have done so without that pump. Nor could I have done so without my husband's constant encouragement.

TUESDAY APRIL 1st

My first experience breastfeeding Michael did not go too well, but it makes me laugh to think of it. He was accustomed to the taste of formula which was much sweeter or at least quite different in taste from breast milk. With the help of a nurse from the maternity floor who was asked to come especially for the occasion, I placed my little baby on a pillow before me as I sat on a rocking chair and positioned him at my breast. He closed his tiny mouth on my rather large nipple, then promptly wrinkled his nose, pulled his head away and clamped his rebellious mouth shut tightly. My God, I thought, he is rejecting me, my soul, my breast and my whole being. I was crushed; I was dismayed that this tiny being so soon was ready to push me away. Nothing, no trick we tried could persuade him. Luckily we had a bottle of breast milk nearby for just such an emergency, but it was the same, Michael rejected both the nipple and the bottle. So we decided that he needed a few trials with breast milk to get him used to it.

WEDNESDAY APRIL 2nd

I decided to go in twice a day to breastfeed him. It was a complicated procedure. Each time, he had to be removed from his oxygen-giving isolette. Then he had to be weighed, both before and after meals, to determine how much fluid he was getting. It was an unreliable measure, but it made the medical staff happy.

After the first dismal trial Michael caught on fast. For me, it was wonderful. Lee always came with me. (I was feeling strange anyway, nursing my baby for the first few times, and to be on stage in the observation nursery compounded my awkwardness and embarrassment.) But I remembered those moments as the happiest that the three of us were to have together. And Lee, well, he watched with pleasure, encouraged and provided support — these were warm and loving times.

THURSDAY APRIL 3rd

After we had breastfed Michael about four times and things began to settle down to a sort of routine, our pattern was disturbed by the sudden appearance one morning, just as I was about to start feeding Michael, of two pediatric cardiologists, a man and a woman who requested they be allowed to, in their words, "watch Michael's behavior at the breast."

Nursing was the one privacy I had been allowed. Yet how could I refuse them this intrusion? They really had me over a barrel; they had control of my son, after all, and I did not dare say no.

My first thoughts were, will Michael and I perform according to their expectations? Will we pass the test? What will they be looking for? Will they be judging my performance also? Will my milk let down with two perfect strangers watching?

In short, this is what happened: Michael, asleep, and I, wide-awake, adrenalin pumping, settled into the armchair; one cardiologist stood to my left, the other to my right. There I was, my breasts full of milk, bare and ready, but Michael slept on. I tried my best to rouse him; he would half open his eyes, only to close them again and slumber on. He would not wake up. Then the female cardiologist broke in, "Now, when you feed this baby, I want to see no fooling around; he must get right down to the business of eating and waste no time outside of his isolette. He must be breathing room air no longer than necessary." Michael remained asleep. Finally, when it became clear that he just wasn't interested in his breakfast that day, the cardiologist asked, "Have you ever breastfed a baby before?" I felt defensive and surprised at the question. "No," I responded truthfully, "this is my first baby." She walked out of the room briskly, leaving me, breasts still bare, sitting in an armchair. As she left she threw over her shoulder, "Well, we shall just have to get someone down here who knows what they're doing."

I sat there for a minute, trying unsuccessfully to regain my dignity and composure, but it was difficult, as I was still half naked, and frightened that every second out of the isolette would bring about Michael's demise. I finally just gave Michael to Lee, stood up, buttoned my blouse and stalked, shaking, out of the nursery, to compose myself in the waiting room, which I supposed was my proper place now that my competency as a mother had been called into question.

Looking back on the incident objectively, I suppose that the cardiologist, puzzled by Michael's symptoms herself, felt uncomfortable in not having any ready answers about his condition, and therefore, felt more at ease accusing *me* of incompetence than herself. At the same time I wondered whether perhaps the woman was unused to dealing with the vagaries of mother love and breastfeeding when perhaps she had taken refuge in the sterility and cut-and-dried security of the medical world. Perhaps she was threatened by the whole scene, never having chosen to have the experience herself.

I was furious. I wanted to scream questions after her: Don't mothers and fathers have any rights when their own child is critically ill? Is nothing sacred? Does the medical staff have to examine, observe and dissect everything? Can I feed my baby only if I measure up to your medical standards of competency? Do I have to go to nursing school to be competent enough to understand what is happening to my child?

FRIDAY APRIL 4th

Michael's condition had not improved; it was his second week of life. He still breathed too fast, and his heart sounds were not good. The cardiologists had decided to perform a more invasive test on him to determine whether there were any structural abnormalities in his heart; the procedure was called cardiac catheterization. They explained it to us briefly; the catheterization required written permission from us, and we had been standing by for two days to give it. A resident from the neonate unit had called us at midnight Thursday night to inform us that they were ready and to get our permission by phone. Apparently he didn't know that a telephoned permission was not legally binding unless it was also telegrammed and witnessed by a third party listening in. Anyway, at midnight Thursday night we all thought that everything was set for Michael to be catheterized the next day.

We waited all day for word from the hospital, expecting any minute word that the test had been completed and perhaps the first results. Late in the afternoon Lee was on the telephone when his call was interrupted on an emergency. Of course he thought that something terrible had happened to Michael and he suffered much unnecessary emotional stress on account of it. The cardiologists had Michael in the laboratory, but had refused to proceed without a telegrammed consent from us, thus, the emergency. Compared to what was to come, this was a very minor mix-up. However, consent duly given properly, the test proceeded. Lee and I waited some more by the phone. Luckily we had some friends with us whom we knew very well.

Finally, three hours after we had telegrammed our consent, Dr. Brown, the cardiologist, called and gave us the horrible and shocking story. Something had gone wrong with the procedure — through a technician's error, an anesthetic called Lidacaine had been injected into Michael's heart instead of dye. His heart had stopped for fifteen minutes. The cardiologists had been able to monitor the circulation and therefore knew exactly how much external cardiac massage to deliver. Dr. Brown said that he thought they had prevented any brain damage, but they couldn't guarantee it. My immediate reaction was to think and say — Oh, Michael, you can have no arms, no legs, but if you have no brain, you're lost!

But Michael was still alive; he needed a respirator to help him breathe; he was on heavy doses of phenobarbital to control convulsions which are a side-effect of Lidacaine; he was on high oxygen and he was placed in the intensive care unit; but, brain-damaged or not, he lived.

With Dr. Brown's immediate admission of error, Lee and I knew we had found someone we could trust. After that we turned often to Dr. Brown because we respected him for his honesty. He also turned out to be our most reliable source of information regarding the details of Michael's care. Without him we would have known very little about the plans the staff had for Michael.

SATURDAY APRIL 5th

The first time we saw Michael after the damaging mishap was heartbreaking. Thursday I had been breastfeeding this adorable little baby of ours, and Saturday he looked near death. He was very pale in comparison to his pinkness of two days before; his head was tipped upwards and there was a tube (endotracheal) stuffed down his throat which delivered oxygen to his lungs and expanded them for him. His hands and feet were tied down to prevent his dislodging his endotracheal tube and his intravenous tube; he was in a drugged stupor from the heavy doses of phenobarbital being given to prevent possible convulsions from the Lidacaine. Michael needed heroic support measures to sustain his life until the effects of the Lidacaine wore off.

I looked at him just once and the tears rolled down my face. I turned away. I could not bear the sight. There was nothing I could do for him.

It was at this time that I first realized that Michael might very well die, and I look back on this day as a turning point in my mind. I began to lose hope. I ceased to be able to see Michael as my adorable brand new first baby. I could not see beyond the tubes which sustained him. Michael became figuratively the property of the intensive care nursery. Even Dr. Cousins, our trusted pediatrician, told us that he was now merely a figure-head, and had no real control over what happened to our son. He was no longer even the physician of record, once Michael had been placed in intensive care.

I knew then that Michael, Lee and I were in for a long haul. I was living literally from moment to moment. I knew that I could not continue for long this way, thinking constantly that good news might break, thinking constantly that Michael would be home with us soon. Michael was in intensive care now. I tried to think now in terms of weeks rather than days. I continued daily entries in my journal because I had a strong intuitive feeling that these days were precious. The journal also helped me to keep a record of events as they happened. My story continues, in narrative form, based on those journal entries.

Coping

In order to deal with our feelings of anxiety over our son's condition and our mutual feelings of impotence and frustration at being unable to help our son grow in any way — at being unable to have any control whatsoever over the details of his care — at being superficial adjuncts to the process of treating him, we took two different tracks which turned out to be mutually beneficial and mutually adaptive.

Lee, an academic by profession, turned to knowledge. Through his reading, intensive study and constant questioning of the medical staff, he kept us both very well informed of every detail of Michael's condition, from blood gas reports to cardiac anatomy and eventually to neuroanatomy. I, on the other hand, and in response to entirely different personal needs, continued milk expression, and tried in other ways to maintain a contact and a relationship with our child. Although it only takes a few seconds to read my brief account of what we did during this time in order to deal with the horrendous strain in our lives, it was a full time job for two intelligent people to stay on top of the situation. It took virtually all of my resources to deal especially with the medical and nursing staff. For one thing, we had to be available at odd times during the day in order to speak to the medical staff about Michael; we could only speak to them when *they* had the time; never did the staff consider that we might not be available to speak to them; and never did they make it easy for us to talk to them, except when they needed permission to perform a medical procedure.

I tried, then, after the cardiac catheterization fiasco, to reconcile myself to the fact that Michael was going to be in that intensive care unit for quite a while longer. I visited him daily. I called to see how he was doing usually twice a day. Michael was being fed intravenously, as the endotracheal tube which helped him breath, made it impossible to feed him by mouth. Later, the order was given to feed him by stomach tube. I continued to express milk into sterile 2 ounce bags, which would then be kept frozen, and thawed to be fed to him by stomach tube. At this point, much to my sadness, there was really nothing I could do except express milk, so I clung to this; I felt useless and cheated and continually anxious and preoccupied. If only someone had told me what to do, even feed my baby by stomach tube, I would have been overjoyed to have a useful and necessary task.

The doctors were still uncertain as to what was wrong with him. His rapid breathing had not diminished; it was therefore decided to keep him on the respirator in a more permanent way. The endotracheal tube was a temporary breathing tube which reached his lungs through his mouth. It was decided to perform a tracheostomy which is a surgical procedure necessitating a slit in his trachea into which would be introduced a plastic tube which would more or less permanently be in his trachea. Permanently, that is, until he did not need it any more. To this tube would be attached hoses delivering oxygen in measured amounts. I was told that it is extremely rare for a baby to have a tracheostomy repair any sooner that six months after it was performed originally, so I knew that Michael would be in the hospital for at least that long. In the back of my mind I also knew that the diagnosis of a possible weakness of the heart muscle due to infection or other cause was by no means certain. Each day I hoped that Michael would improve, and each day I called the hospital before visiting only to discover that basically Michael's condition remained unchanged. Except for minor variations in the respirator settings or small changes in the amount of breast milk he was allowed, Michael's care remained the same. The nurses changed shifts every eight or twelve hours and I got to know some of them a little. They were responsible for carrying out the orders regarding Michael's basic care. I took each day as it came, as much as possible. I lived from one visit to the next, as if the visits were the only real events in my life.

The fact that Lee and I wanted detailed information on Michael's care was a surprise to the nurses. One of them even tried to hide Michael's chart from Lee, saying, when he asked for it, that it was "where it belonged" (in a drawer, out of sight). We were told that "Most parents were not in the least interested in blood gas reports, respiratory rate, or the number of times the baby vomited during the night." But Lee insisted on having access to the chart. He was not like "most parents" in this respect. Both of us resented deeply being stereotyped in this way. We both found ourselves feeling defensive about wanting medical information.

Dr. Brown was a rare exception to what I have said previously about the people we encountered in the medical world. He was an extremely reliable source of information. We usually spent an hour with him once a week, during which time we asked all the questions we had stored up in our minds. He answered all of the ones he could in great detail, and he was quick to admit if he was not able to answer them. Always during these weekly sessions we wanted to ask what were Michael's chances for survival, and if he survived, would he be disabled in any way? These were the questions that Dr. Brown could not answer. He still maintained that Michael probably had a viral infection of the heart muscle, and to this end X-rays were taken every few days to see if his heart size had decreased, indicating that the infection had subsided. Always during our meetings, Dr. Brown gave us the latest results, and always they were the same, no change in heart size. Lee and I always hoped for good news. We were constantly on tenterhooks. Dr. Brown never let us give up hope, nor did we want to.

Nonetheless, Lee and I had good reason to doubt the competency of even so great an institution as this intensive care unit — the error during the cardiac catheterization — the sloppy administration of the consent forms for that test — and the occasional misinformation we were given by the resident on duty in the unit. Because this was our son, and because the doctors did not seem to be able to give us any firm answers, Lee and I on more than one occasion had cause to question the actions taken by the intensive care unit staff regarding Michael.

Cause to Question

One incident was particularly frightening. Michael's condition when he was five weeks old warranted frequent blood tests. His blood gas levels indicated how well or how poorly his heart was functioning. The tests caused the red blood count to decrease faster than his body could replace it. At some point we knew that he would require a transfusion. In addition to this impending transfusion, Michael was due for yet another attempt at breathing without the help of the respirator.

This was the situation one Friday in early May when Lee and I had one of our talks with Dr. Brown. Dr. Brown told us that Michael was to have a transfusion that afternoon, and he was careful and considerate to warn us that the extra blood in his system would exacerbate his symptoms — fluid retention and rapid breathing. As we drove home that day we were not particularly worried, and we were glad that the oxygen-carrying ability of his blood was to be improved. Around eight that night we called to see how Michael was tolerating the transfusion. We were told that no transfusion had occurred. This puzzled us, as Dr. Brown had seemed so sure that Michael was to be transfused that day.

The following morning, when I went to visit him, I was greeted at the door by a nurse, all smiles, telling me that Michael had again been taken off the respirator and was trying to breath on his own. I hid my alarm, but I was very concerned that they had taken Michael off the respirator when a transfusion was imminent. Both actions at once would most certainly put his heart in jeopardy. I felt that the doctors were not giving Michael every chance to succeed off the respirator. I was both angry and alarmed. I had no illusions this time of hope for Michael's success. I went home, and Lee and I tried to get hold of Dr. Brown, but of course, it being Saturday, he was unavailable. There was nothing to do but watch helplessly the following sequence of events — Sunday, Michael needed frequent suctioning to remove fluid from his lungs; he was breathing rapidly and with difficulty; he was tired and could hardly eat. Sunday night he was given a slow transfusion. Monday he was even more tired and his breathing was more labored. So we were not surprised when by Tuesday Michael was put back on the respirator; his congestive symptoms had been aggravated by the transfusion. We finally got in touch with Dr. Brown who was as surprised as we were that Michael had been taken off the respirator. We had called the resident on duty and asked him why this had been done. His reply was that it seemed like a good thing to do at the time! He sounded so cavalier about it — I wish someone had consulted us first!

Apparently the administrative set-up could not prevent this sort of thing happening because Dr. Brown, a pediatric cardiology fellow, acted in an advisory capacity on Michael's case; the final decisions were made by the intensive care unit staff. The resident on duty often made decisions such as the one to take Michael off the respirator; however, the resident was still only a doctor in training. Lee and I could not understand why, if the consensus was that Michael was a heart patient, the ICU did not take the advice of the cardiologists more seriously. We made an appointment with the Director of the unit and questioned him about this. He replied that in the future he would try to increase communication between the cardiologists and the intensive-care unit staff. His answer hardly placated us, but under the circumstances we could not have accomplished more. Michael's pediatrician was right; he had advised us prior to this meeting that doctors do not like to be questioned on medical matters by laymen and that we had better restrict our comments to a criticism of the administration of the ICU rather than a criticism of the medical decisions made by the staff. This was a very difficult interview to conduct, but I thought that Lee had done so with great tact and delicacy.

The upshot of this interview with the Director was that our complaint got back to the resident in charge of the unit who then had a discussion with Dr. Brown, and asked him not to talk to us any more about Michael's care because it was confusing us! It seemed then that given the facts we were still stereotyped into "confused" parents. Implied was the comment that the less we knew about the better. I hope that it is clear what we were up against in our search for straight answers and information. I hope that it is also clear how, when faced with hard lay questions regarding medical decisions, the medical profession closed in its ranks. Dr. Cousins, Michael's pediatrician, too, had received a call from someone in the unit who begged him to head off our queries. The staff just didn't know what to do about us, he was told. To our relief and satisfaction, Dr. Cousins stood up for us, replying that the fault was not by any means with us, but lay with the administration of the unit. He said, "There's nothing wrong with them! Any problems that you have are of your own making!" Had not Dr. Cousins supported us, who knows just how awful it might have been!

Perhaps in an attempt to deal with their own anxieties in relating to a mother and a critically ill infant, or perhaps in a misguided attempt to help, it was not unusual for hospital personnel to tell us their own tales of sadness and despair. If I could pick one of the sequence of events as a crowning blow, a last straw, it would be the following. Tuesday night after the mix-up in the transfusion I went in the see Michael. The excerpt from my journal speaks for itself.

> "He's back on the respirator as of 4:30 p.m. at two breaths per minute, 40% oxygen – he looks O.K. colorwise, but his legs lie limp. He's awake and lookin' all around with his big blue eyes. An older nurse is taking care of him. She is giving him his first feeding by bottle, as he's been too tired to suck all day. He's been throwing up too and they've had to suction his lungs much more frequently.
>
> Damn it – I could have told them this would happen on Sunday!
>
> Nurse tells me that cardiac babies make up with their eyes what they can't do with their arms and legs. That they're smart and never miss a trick with their eyes; whereas other babies spend so much time moving around and sucking their thumbs that they miss a lot that is going on around them. Then she told me of her little niece who had an operation for patent ductus and lived to the age of three years.
>
> I tried to be nice and said well, at least if Michael dies I will have done everything I could to make his stay here happy.

This only egged her on.

Meanwhile, she's feeding Michael the bottle while he's lying on his side in bed — not in her arms — she's clucking and cooing over him and doing all the mothering herself — and I want to wring her neck as I stand by watching and feeling as if *my* brand of mothering isn't good enough, and it really is the only thing I have to offer him that until this moment gives me pleasure too. And she is taking it all away.

I did not return to the hospital for five days after this. My milk supply reached dangerously low levels, because I felt superfluous and I was discouraged. I wished this horrible suspense of not knowing whether Michael would live or die would end. I became so desperately unhappy that I truly believed that I wanted him to die. I wished desperately that he would live, and I also wished that he would die. The two desires lived constantly in my mind side by side. I felt shattered. I was deeply angry. I wanted to hit people. More and more during the month of June, my thoughts turned to death. I began thinking about euthanasia and wondered if it was a possibility in Michael's case. I had heard that there are some babies two years old who never have been off a respirator. I could not stand it that long. But, I realized that if this came to pass, I would have to stand it as I had done so far. I was in continual misery. I gave up milk expression and tried to appreciate Michael as much as I could. He was still fun to hold, even though he still only weighed seven pounds.

Toward the end of June we found out that Michael was going to die. The doctors had discovered that he had massive arterio-veinous malformations in the midbrain. An operation would leave him a vegetable for a few years, but the malformations would eventually reform, and he would die. The neurosurgeons advised against operating. He had never had a chance from the second month of his in utero development on. We were told that Michael had at most six months to live.

The sudden spectre of my baby's certain death frightened, shocked and awed me. I did not feel relief. I wanted to stay away from Michael — to begin to forget (I thought) right away. I did not want to see him again. But I woke up one morning after about two days with the sudden realization that the fact he was to die didn't really change anything. He had not died yet! I knew that I would forever regret it if I did not make the utmost of the precious time we had left together. So I continued to go and visit him every day.

On one of those days, I was called into the Director's office. The resident in charge was there also. The Director told me in a long speech that the unit had done everything possible for my baby. No further therapeutic procedures would help him recover. I was told that in cases like this there are considered two parallel factors — the patient and the parents. I was terrified — frozen in fear — during the interview. It seemed so vague as to what exactly was expected of me, and this frightened me more. I did not want to watch Michael fade, sicken, suffer and die. I was very frightened of this too. We were moving out of state in one month, and I told the Director that if Michael were still alive, I could not leave him here, but would have to take him to another ICU in the town in which we were to live. I did not want Michael to suffer in a prolonged, futile struggle when all he could ever hope to have would be more of the same. This was all I could convey to the two doctors. I told them that my husband's feelings were much the same. In the end any decisions that might or might not be made were left up to the intensive care unit and to the natural course of Michael's illness. It seemed unfair that the only time that anyone in the hospital was interested in my thoughts and feelings about Michael's care was in regards to his death.

I urged Lee to come with me to see Michael for the same reasons that I went to see him, and toward the end, Lee did come. We took pictures and I fed Michael his beets. His dietary restrictions were lifted, and for a few days he drank lots of formula and we all spoiled him as much as we could. One of the nurses brought him a baseball cap that said Junior League on it. He looked adorable and he just loved his meals.

At home we always waited for the phone to ring with the final news. I hoped it would not happen that way, but that we would get some warning. I began to think of burial and where it should be.

One day we called the hospital to inquire after Michael, and the resident in charge told us that he had just given Michael some morphine, as he was extremely uncomfortable, struggling for air. Lee and I let an hour go by before we went to the hospital to give the morphine a chance to take effect. Michael was white. He lay limp on his pillow with his eyes opening and closing slowly. Lee said that he was cold to the touch. I took one look and covered my eyes— he was so obviously dying. No one spoke to us and no one looked up when we entered the nursery. All we could hear were the machines bubbling and sighing — and Michael lay white on his bed. I didn't think he'd last the night. It was very quiet.

We left the hospital. We didn't know what to do with ourselves, not wanting to go home for the inevitable phone call. Finally we went home and the resident called to tell us that Michael had died ten minutes after we left. We were shaking inside.

CHAPTER
6

Dignity of Person in the Final Phase of Life: An Exploratory Study*

Mary Louise Nash

A prolonged period of dying in an institution is becoming part of the life cycle for more and more persons. Over two-thirds of all deaths occur today in hospitals, nursing homes, or other similar facilities [1]. In the past it was often possible to prepare at home for a "good" death, with the help of those who belonged to the family circle. Today, however, as the dying process has moved from the family setting into the public sphere, the dying person is physically and psychologically removed from his own circle and even from himself. Many persons are finally awakening to what this imposes on our dying people and how it deprives the living as well of invaluable human experiences. The highly personal, deeply intense experience of dying has become increasingly encased within the technological procedures of life-saving and life-extending. The patient's values, spoken by others if expressed at all, compete with the values of the institution [2].

The "secularization" of modern culture relates to our difficulty dealing with death. What is valued is the work of the ruling generation — the vigorous, the productive! Our energies appear invested in a "high noon" vision of the human condition and, consequently, there is avoidance of persons whose lives are

* An earlier version of this chapter was presented at the National Conference of Social Welfare, San Francisco, May 14, 1975. This study was facilitated by the support of CARCOA (Communities Associated for Research and Care of the Aged).

marked strongly by suffering, aging or death [3]. Frequently it is said that it is not death which is feared, nor the pain associated with the physical condition. Rather, it is being relegated to the periphery; it is the loneliness, the indignity so frequently associated with the dying process [4]. These observations are of special significance in our American society, where there is an increasing tendency to segregate the elderly and to hospitalize or isolate the dying.

The great advances made in the past fifty or so years in medicine have been revolutionary and have, along with other developments, greatly influenced our attitudes toward death. In the United States, premature death is no longer imminent. In 1900, 16 per cent of all deaths were of persons over sixty-five years of age. In 1970, persons over sixty-five comprised 70 per cent of the total number of deaths [5]. Illness and death are the object of an empirical knowledge and an activity which have clearly been proved effective generally. However, the success of medical science in prolonging life, along with the astonishing achievements of man in outer space, have to be matched by an educational revolution affecting his inner space also. A new union of science and spirituality is the main challenge posed to those who seek a revitalization of quality of life.

Statement of the Problem

Patients who are in terminal illness or in the last phase of their lives are not just dying. They are also living. Whether or not they have the opportunity to live this final human experience to the fullest is influenced in great measure by the environment and persons who take care of them [6]. The fulfillment of a person's biological needs is definable and concrete. However, the characteristics which make him human — his relatedness and feelings — are much more abstract, less concrete, and more difficult of definition. Yet it is the resolution of these needs which essentially gives meaning to life.

Helping the dying person to live out the last issues and weeks of life with dignity is the focus of much of Kubler-Ross's works [7]. The importance of relatively open and candid communication between the hospital staff, the patient and the family is a central theme in her interaction with dying patients. From interviews with dying patients she describes the five "stages" through which the patient moves that help us to understand the process of dying. However, despite Kubler-Ross's important contribution, it is apparent that all persons do not progress through the five stages. Hinton reports that about one-half of the persons dying in a general hospital eventually come to acknowledge openly and to accept the end of their life, a quarter express distress, another fourth say little about it [8]. Weisman and Kastenbaum indicate that the person in the hospital is likely to become "a patient," a specific social role, and attention needs to be given to other roles significant to the patient so that his identity is not diminished [9]. They note that "Many aged people suffer from devaluation, not disease" [9, p. 37].

Therefore, with a growing proportion of persons likely to die in hospitals or similar institutions, it is of primary importance that the healing professions become more fully aware of their special opportunity and responsibility to promote dignity of life in the time period prior to death. Salient to the issue is the question: What kinds of situations tend to maintain and foster or, on the other hand, diminish the dignity or quality of life in a person whose death is imminent? Data that could be helpful in exploring this question were collected through a series of personal interviews with persons who themselves were in terminal illness and/or dying.

Methodology

This exploratory study was an attempt to identify the factors affecting the "dignity" of a person's life through unstructured personal interviews with patients in the advanced or terminal phase of their illness; that is, their disease was considered irreversible and treatment was designed to ameliorate whatever discomfort occurred. Twenty-four patients comprised the sample, ranging in age from thirty-six to ninety; two-thirds of them were over sixty-five years of age. All were residents of a 2,000 bed chronic care institution in a large metropolitan area. Three to ten interviews were held with each person, a total of 140 interviews.

The time this longitudinal interview technique absorbed and the slow pace at which the data were acquired can best be justified by the need for flexibility and time to develop a relationship with a patient to the level of sufficient trust (where concern for the other is communicated) so that sharing of feeling can occur. The term "unstructured" interview is somewhat deceptive for this type of interview was by no means lacking in structure. However, in contrast to the structured interview, it offered considerable freedom in the questioning procedure and emphasized the informant's world of meaning. The fundamental goal of each interview was to record what transpired in the patient's own words and to be sensitive to gestural and verbal cues indicating that a given incident carried significant meanings for the respondent. The investigator communicated with each individual patient that, "I would very much like you to help me understand what you are experiencing." Recording was done as soon as possible following each session.

The analysis of interviews involved a process of transforming interview content into symbols which could be tabulated and coded. The 140 interviews were analyzed for descriptions of behavior responses clear enough to facilitate an inference. These accounts of behavior, totaling 126, were abstracted and sorted according to dignity or lack of dignity inferred. For the purposes of this study, the investigator as the single rater, relied on face validity to assess whether or not desired results had been obtained [10]. In subsequent studies additional raters should be used. Responses classified under dignity were few, only twelve (10%) of the 126 behavior accounts; the remaining 114 (90%) were considered to be incongruent with dignity. These 114 responses were further classified under four themes most frequently expressed (or referred to) in interview sessions: pain, loss, loneliness, intrusiveness.

The concept of "dignity" encompasses a special concern for the quality of life and can be defined and explored from various perspectives. However, within the context of this study, "dignity" refers to those characteristics of a person and the environment which allow him to feel an identity, a sense of self worth, a sense of stature. In other words, the patient moves toward death in an environment which promotes an inward feeling of goodness, of self-respect, and enhances the meaning of the person's life. The behavior reflects a concept of self as being worthy, capable of being liked for himself.

On the other hand, a lack of dignity — to feel helpless, hopeless or alien — is synonymous with feeling powerless, out of control, and distanced from those people and situations which provide a sense of stability, of security, of well-being. There is movement toward disaffection, dissolution and resignation — qualities not congruent with dignity and caring. The behavior reflects a concept of self as hopeless, damaged, deformed or alien.

Summary of Findings

The twelve (10%) behavior accounts classified under dignity are those where the patient is involved with persons, family members and/or staff, in decision making or other positive forms of relatedness as inferred from interview responses. In the following situation the behavior of this sixty-four-year-old woman is expressive of distress, yet reflects a sense of relatedness.

> Pt: (Starting to cry — did not talk for a few minutes.) "I'll never return home. My husband can talk about it now. Did you see him? If only you knew how grateful I am that the doctors were so truthful with me — told me everything except time . . ." (Crying)

> Int: "You can talk about this with your husband — how you feel?"

> Pt: "I tell him to get a smaller place to live — like the special places for old people — so someone will check on him. He doesn't want to think I'm not coming back home."

The importance of intact positive human relationships has been underscored in a number of studies [7, 11]. The dignity possible to the dying person is part of the meaningful interaction of the person and one or more participants. In general, dying people have the desire to remain in contact with everyday life, and the loss of the ability to relate and to love lowers the capacity to be involved and diminishes the sense of control.

Reflections of patients demonstrated that purposeful consideration of patient involvement was usually absent. Expectations for the patient to assume a passive role are so strong in our society, that often the person feels he has no right for decision making concerning his own life, or to even ask questions. Yet not to allow or provide for the patient's participation in decision making is to force or encourage dependency, to promote isolation, and to undermine the patient's self-esteem.

In situations rated low in dignity, patients appear weary, isolated, apathetic, indifferent and resigned to their coming death. This resignation can best be described as a "defeatism" and diminishes for them their sense of being valued or "cared" about for themselves. In these situations the patients verbalized concern about their pain and loneliness; others expressed concerns related to the themes of intrusiveness and loss. An interpretation of each of the four themes follows.

PAIN

A significant factor of pain is the terrible loneliness. Each person has his own unique pain, a pain which is indescribable to anybody else. Thirty-eight (30%) of the interview responses reflected this feeling. Patients gave examples of asking for pain medication and receiving as a sole response: "It's not time yet." This was often perceived by the patients as staff not understanding the pain they were experiencing. The feeling expressed in the following fifty-two-year-old woman's statement was typical of many.

"I get concerned about having to ask for pain medication and for help. Maybe they think I don't need all the medication — that I'm really not that sick. It's so hard to have to ask."

The patient needs to believe that staff do understand and really want to do something about the pain. Frequently nursing personnel express concern over "addictive" problems. One student told the investigator that she was upset having to give morphine to a fifty-four-year-old man dying of cancer. "Nothing was important to him except the morphine." She said it was difficult for her to offer it every third hour as it was ordered, so she always waited until he asked. There is, of course, the possibility of mismanagement of medication by over-sedating the patient. However, the frequently used method of withholding a drug until pain becomes severe serves to increase the pain further by anxiety and tension. If a patient continually has to ask for relief, he is far more likely to become dependent upon the drug and the person who gives it to him, and less likely to maintain his independence and dignity [6].

Adequate control of pain and other physical distress can reduce and/or relieve the patient's tension or acute anxiety and free him from concentration on his physical problems [12]. Then the person is more apt to have the freedom to be aware of his own personhood, of others, and of his environment.

LONELINESS

The feeling of loneliness was the theme of twenty-five (20%) of the patients' perceptions as contained in the interview situations. It was expressed more often by patients seventy years and over than by those in the younger age groupings. There are undoubtedly several reasons, but what is significant is the "estimated social value" of the dying patient [13]. Social value is usually determined by such characteristics as age, intelligence, occupation, family position and beauty. An elderly dying person appears to receive low priority both emotionally and functionally, as the staff attempt to cope with other nursing situations.

The feeling of loneliness seemed intensified by immobility. This is described by an eighty-three-year-old woman, severely crippled by arthritis:

> "It is terrible not to be able to move. It takes two nurses to lift me to the other side. And it's terrible when I need a bedpan. I'm such a burden. I lie here thinking all kinds of things. I'm so lonely. Nobody wants me. I'm by myself. Just look at me."
>
> "I feel so alone – just forgotten. But I know I'm not. My niece does so much for me, but she can never stay long – she's always so busy. Sometimes I cry and there's no one even to know."

Loneliness is not so much the result of social isolation or a lessening of social contacts, but rather a rupture in one's history, a cutting away of meaningful ties. For the personnel or family members who are not comfortable with their own feelings about the dying process, behavior toward the patient will likely take on various forms of denial or avoidance. When this occurs, chances for a relationship to develop which enables the patient to share his inner concerns in unlikely. The resulting isolation of the patient is described by one author as equivalent to being driven from the social community, a premature burial [14].

Although ultimately each person dies alone, this does not preclude the real possibility of others sharing in the patient's dying experience. Only then is emotional expression rather than emotional repression more apt to occur.

INTRUSIVENESS

For the conscious and mentally alert patient, the concept of intrusiveness is significant to his sense of possessing or losing control. This was apparent in fifteen (12%) of the behavior responses. Patients' rights are so frequently related in our thinking to tremendous legal decisions. Sometimes, however, they are what one significant helping family member or one staff member does in a single minute to help a patient feel there are controls that he has a right to, up to the moment of death. Persons ministering to the patient can focus so narrowly on the task to be rendered that other more human characteristics of the patient are excluded. The following words of a seventy-five-year-old man with cancer of the prostate convey feelings of becoming more a case of disease and less a person.

> "I don't know why God gave this to me. It's like having big needles stuck deep within me . . . and the girls come in to irrigate the tube – and they push the water in – and the pain is just so terrible. It doesn't bother them to hurt me. No one seems to care or know how I feel."

A form of anticipatory guidance should be part of each step in care: "I want to turn you on your side, Mr._____ , and irrigate your catheter. May I do that?" The "may I" is important with any procedure or for any service which intrudes not only on a patient's body, but on his time as well, as it helps the patient feel he has some control of the situation. One patient told a student who was consciously trying to use this approach, "I have the feeling that I could stop you if I wanted to." And this, at the simplest, most basic level, is what is meant by the right to dignity and self-respect.

LOSS

Although specifics of situations were different, and the physical condition, cognitive ability and usual level of responsiveness to environment of each patient was not known, the majority of patients shared in common a high level of psychosocial stress by having to cope simultaneously with several serious problems involving loss. This was revealed in thirty-six (29%) of the accounts and is illustrated in the following situation.

> Pt: "I want to go home. I can take the pain pills at home like I do here."
>
> Int: "Do you think you can manage?"
>
> Pt: "Won't know unless I try. I managed before. Of course my husband is sick now." (Patient leaned forward and whispered): "You know that he has a tumor, too." (Started to cry.) "It's hard. My daughter is back from Germany and goes to Kentucky next week . . . They say I can't go back to my apartment — not even to try to see if it will work — not even to pack things away. I'm not even 65." (Patient's husband had diagnosis of cancer of prostate and died shortly after this interview.)

As patients become bound to their bodies by their illness, independence and its mobility diminishes and the persons literally lose control of their own lives.

Patients who suffer a physical change incur an additional kind of personal loss of varied intensity. One patient, whose lower half of face was swollen and disfigured from extensive cancer of the tongue and mouth, manifested a pervasive anxiety by expressing over and over a feeling of being rejected by his family and by the staff because of his "ugly disease." An important consequence is that this person, perceiving his cancer as destroying his physical image, experiences himself in a social and psychological isolation at a time when he is very much in need of significant human relationships.

Much of the behavior we take as "bad aging" can be understood in terms of bereavement overload [15]. Often one loss follows another before the elder can pull through his mourning process, and there are seldom opportunities to mourn for or replenish what or who has been lost. Consider the prospect of death when "defeat" resulting from a series of losses for which there is no compensation, is compounded by the deterioration of disease. For example, the only audible response of one patient in an interview session was, "I'm finished." This elderly person's one arm was secured for an intravenous. His other arm was restrained, allowing a very minimal range of motion.

Discussion

The purpose of this exploratory study was to identify the kinds of situations which influence the "dignity" of the person who is living out the final phase of life. Of the 126 accounts of behavior abstracted from personal interviews, only twelve (10%) of them were classified as revealing a sense of dignity of self-respect. The concept, "dignity," regardless of its ambiguity, stands partly for the proposition that there are more or less dignified ways to face the end of life. The possibilities of dying with a sense of dignity can be diminished, undermined, or perhaps eliminated in various ways by persons in the environment. The overall majority of the behavioral accounts (90%) were considered incongruent with dignity; that is, they reflected a sense of the patient feeling powerless and out of control. These responses were further classified according to four themes emerging from the nature of the content: pain, loneliness, intrusiveness and loss, and can be summarized as distinct, yet interrelated concepts.

PAIN, not controlled or understood, lessens the sense of security and
confidence in self.
Feelings of unrelatedness deepen the pain of LONELINESS.
INTRUSIVENESS diminishes a sense of control over one's life.
Compounding and overlapping effects of multiple LOSS lead to
bereavement overload.

Results of the study demonstrate the necessity to promote consciousness-raising of health personnel about human needs of persons who are in the final phase of their lives. Awareness of relatedness and feelings of persons in the time of life before death is not only unique to members of the health profession, but to all who interact with the dying.

However, in view of the increasing number of deaths that occur each year in hospitals and health-related institutions, and considering that health professionals, especially nurses, determine to a large extent how people live through their final days, education to respond more fully to human needs of the dying becomes a pressing reality. While nurses have a strong influence on dying patients, as well as on their family and friends, it is well-documented that many of them are apprehensive in death-related situations and tend to avoid and withdraw [16]. Nurses do not escape the teachings of their culture, nor do the institutions within which they function.

The concept of multiple loss is not only relevant to individual patients unable to mobilize their own resources for coping with loss. It also applies to personnel who work in a context of many losses or, in other words, where there is a high rate of death. They can easily defend themselves by hiding behind a detached professional facade. In other words, it is possible for them to practice social isolation in their contacts with difficult and disturbing patients in order to protect themselves from unresolved feelings of loss and grief and psychological pain.

The relationship between education and human qualities must receive more attention at all levels, in all disciplines. This does not necessarily mean we need new courses, but rather a re-education of our attitudes toward life and toward death [17]. This educational challenge has never been more acute, clear, nor more apparent than it is today.

REFERENCES

1. M. Lerner, When, Why and Where People Die, in: *The Dying Patient,* (ed. Brim, Freeman, Levine and Scotch), Russell Sage Foundation, New York, p. 7, 1970.
2. E. Cassell, Dying in a Technological Society, *Hastings Center Studies, II,* pp. 31-36, May 1974.
3. R. Kastenbaum, . . . Gone Tomorrow, *Geriatrics,* pp. 127-134, November, 1974.
4. E. Marcovitz, What is the Meaning of Death to the Dying Person and His Survivors, *Omega, 4:*1, p. 14, 1973.
5. R. S. Morison, Dying, *Scientific American, CCXXIX,* pp. 55-62, September, 1973.
6. C. Saunders, The Last Stages of Life, *American Journal of Nursing, LXV,* pp. 70-75, March, 1965.
7. E. Kubler-Ross, *On Death and Dying,* Macmillan Co., Inc., New York, 1969.
8. J. Hinton, *Dying,* Penguin Books, Baltimore, 1967.
9. A. Weisman and R. Kastenbaum, *The Psychological Autopsy: A Study of the Terminal Phase of Life,* Community Mental Health Journal, Monograph No. 4, Behavioral Publications, Inc., New York, 1968.
10. B. Berelson, *Content Analysis in Communication Research,* Behavior Publishing, Inc., New York, 1972.
11. A. D. Weisman, *On Dying and Denying: A Psychiatric Study of Terminality,* Behavioral Publications, Inc., New York, 1972.
12. C. Saunders, The Patients Response to Treatment, in: *Catastrophic Illness in the Seventies: Critical Issues and Complex Decisions,* Proceedings of the Fourth National Symposium, Cancer Care, Inc., New York, pp. 33-46, 1971.
13. B. Glaser and A. Strauss, *Awareness of Dying,* Aldine Publishing Co., Chicago, 1965.
14. W. F. May, The Social Power of Death in Contemporary Experience, *Social Research, XXXIX,* pp. 463-488, 1972.
15. R. Kastenbaum, Epilogue, in: *The Psychology of Adult Development and Aging,* (ed. C. Eisdorfer and M. P. Lawton), American Psychological Association, Washington, D. C., p. 705, 1973.
16. J. Quint, *The Nurse and the Dying Patient,* Macmillan Co., Inc., New York, 1967.
17. W. Shibles, *Death: An Interdisciplinary Analysis,* The Language Press, Whitewater, Wisconsin, 1974.

PART 2
Survivors
of
Death

The dying and death of one person affects many others. In fact, research has consistently shown that the single greatest loss that concerns people regarding their own deaths is the effect on those they love. When you die, your dying process and death will affect your family members, many of your friends, your co-workers and others with whom you have working relationships, members of organizations to which you belong, and so forth. For some of these individuals, losing you would make only a slight difference, but others would mourn your loss for a long time.

Grief and bereavement do not necessarily begin at the time the loss occurs, since we can anticipate and plan for the death. As Fulton and Fulton explore, this anticipatory grieving has substantial advantages as well as some difficulties. But the sudden and unexpected deaths, discussed in the Vollman et al and Markusen et al chapters, are usually much more disruptive for survivors than deaths for which we have time to plan. Sudden and unexpected deaths are especially cruel to the survivors, and sudden infant deaths that seem to appear from nowhere and strike the helpless and innocent baby can be especially cruel.

For the most part, the best healing for such losses is time and the opportunity to feel the grief and sadness. Sometimes the power of the loss is too great, and the bereaved person does not move through the pain, but remains in some fashion still in the pain. Perhaps the shock of the death was so great that the person's denial of its reality has never really ceased. Perhaps there was so much unfinished business with the dead person that it seems impossible that the relationship no longer exists as it once existed. Psychotherapy can be helpful in coping with these pathological responses to death and loss, but in most circumstances, the best support system is the familiar network of friends, family, neighbors, and others who were there previously.

For many of us, the first experience of significant loss is the death of a grandparent, and our response to this loss is a function of the length and intensity of the relationship, our own age, and personality and the behavior of those who are important to us. Not infrequently, however, the first meaningful death is that of a pet, and this often is an effective beginning to the understanding of death. Unfortunately, some adults under-estimate the importance of this death or they try to quickly to find a substitute (this would be like a just-widowed mother marrying right away to get a father for her children), without permitting an adequate time for grieving.

Just as we encourage ways of relating to the dying person so that he or she does not feel abandoned, it is important that the survivors of death also have people available so that they do not feel abandoned. And it is also important that we realize that the impact of a serious loss does not disappear in two or three weeks. In fact, it is becoming increasingly evident that we may continue to grieve the death (or loss through divorce) of a parent or a very close person years and even decades later.

CHAPTER
7

Shouldering
a
Burden[1]

Kathy Calkins [2]

The time and effort involved in caring for a chronically ill, aged, or dying relative often constitute a burden on the patient's family. I shall primarily address the burden of day-to-day *custodial care*, which is imposed when the patient is unable to perform care-taking tasks himself. Family members generally think of such responsibilities as a burden—although, when confronted themselves with the specific obligations of caring for a close relative, especially a spouse, they may not admit such feelings, or admit them only long after the relative is gone.

Close kinship ties and proximity of residence form the initial *conditions* under which relatives assume the burden of care. The availability of a supporting relative and the patient's consciousness of his situation are important determinants in how long care is *maintained* at home. *Re-evaluation* of whether the burden can be continued to be shouldered tends to occur at points when the patient's physical condition worsens. Then, after the care is *relinquished* to professionals, the family's burden shifts to handling the further duties and ambiguities surrounding death. Each of these phases will be explicated in this chapter.

METHODS AND DATA

Care of the dying patient within the context of noninstitutionalized arrangements will be examined within a sociological framework. In contrast to other studies, such as Anselm L. Strauss' and Barney G. Glaser's recent works on long-term dying in a hospital setting (1965, 1968, and 1970), and David Sudnow's (1967) report on the social organization of dying, my investigation was focused on home care provided until the final stages of the patient's dying trajectory.

The data were collected through interviews and informal observations conducted with local medical professionals and relatives of patients who were dying or who had recently died. Much of the data was drawn from interviews with approximately 20 working-class and lower middle-class families whose dying member finally had been admitted to a nearby county hospital; I was particularly interested in the perspectives and

[1] The research reported here was supported by Russell Sage Foundation Grant #445210-58072, awarded to Anselm L. Strauss, University of California, San Francisco.
[2] The author wishes to thank Anselm Strauss for his interest and help during both the field work and writing phases of this report. Barney Glaser and Roger Pritchard also deserve thanks for their cogent reviews of earlier drafts.

circumstances of these kinsmen, since little is known about their relationship to the dying process. Four of these families were Black, two were Mexican American, and the remainder were White. Comparative material was collected from middle-class families concerning the care they gave to their dying relatives. The methodology for the research is based upon Grounded Theory, as elaborated by sociologists Glaser and Strauss in their recent book (1967). The Grounded Theory approach emphasizes the discovery of concepts and theory through systematic analysis of the data, rather than the logical deductive theoretical formulations of other approaches. Since the data themselves provide the source of the emerging conceptual framework, systematic coding and categorizing of it starts at the beginning of data collection. Initial categories and conjectures are then subject to hypothesis testing while the researcher is still doing field work so that he may better discover the conditions under which his emerging categories are operant. The researcher clarifies his analysis by writing notes on the properties of his categories. The integration of these notes shows the interrelationships of the theoretical framework while, simultaneously, rendering and synthesizing the data.

ASSUMING THE BURDEN

The Development of Burdens

A family can provide for a patient in several ways—by giving money, time, space or care. Whether a family will undertake the actual care of a patient is related to the other kinds of burdens and the extent to which they can be evaluated by the family. When family members can directly assess aspects of the burdens confronting themselves, they may intentionally decide to *assume* the burdens, *assign* them to specific family members, or *delegate* them to outside agencies. When direct evaluation is improbable, or the family is relatively unaware of the circumstances which they are confronting, such decisions are apt to be forced by medical circumstances. Furthermore, the events leading to choices may occur either so imperceptibly, or for that matter so quickly, that the family may remain unaware of how the decision is actually made.

In the beginning, the family's burdens are likely to be those of money and time, rather than housing and care. Gradual increments in attention and assistance may be made for the older and dying relative. Within the normal processes of the life cycle, as individuals retire from work, children and grandchildren may give greater time to their surviving older relatives. The family assumes chores and tasks as tokens of their interest and devotion, but frequently such symbolic gestures come to be relied upon. For example, gardening duties may be taken over by a grandson when his grandfather dies, as a gesture of his concern for his grandmother. At the time this is done, the only necessity may be the symbolic meaning, which may rapidly change to a condition contingent for maintaining the living arrangement of the older person. Shifts from attention and assistance tend to occur: These form a sequential pattern of giving greater amounts of care.

The course of deterioration necessarily affects the kinds of burdens these relatives are forced to shoulder. Two major patterns were discovered in the data. In the first, the chronic illness pattern, the family stressed the disease process. The chronically-ill person was viewed as a patient. He and his illness were so intertwined that no consideration of him could be made without it; the illness had become merged with his identity. In addition to becoming a focal point of family interaction, the illness became a basis of the life style of the family members (Cf. Davis, 1963:162). Thus, the burden of care is something that everyone is aware of. It cannot be overlooked or denied. Under these circumstances, the burden of care may inundate the entire family (Davis, 1964:123). The strain of continuous care leads family members tacitly or openly to define their relative as a burden.

The other major pattern is the gradual-aging pattern in which the ill or aged person is viewed by his family as slowly growing older and less able to help himself. Age rather than illness is at the foreground both of his existence and the family's life style. Hence, only sporadically does the illness become the major focus of attention. The burdens on the family are not dissimilar from the occasional acute illnesses of younger family members, since their frequency and duration may not seriously disrupt ongoing family relationships. Moreover, family members prefer to treat critical incidents in the health of the gradually-aging person as acute episodes from which recovery is assumed. In this pattern, the phasing of chronic illness is likely to remain somewhat obscured. The gradual-aging pattern may be transformed, however, into the chronic-illness pattern if the person suffers a major complication such as a stroke or heart attack. Then the family may have to define the burdens differently in light of the new contingencies.

Professionals often are instrumental in defining the kinds of burdens the family is going to have, as well as predicting new ones. When professionals urge families to change the ill person's accommodations, it is usually in anticipation that the type of care required will cause the family greater burdens than they could reasonably shoulder. The social workers whom I interviewed confer with families about changes when a relative's care requires continual observation, lifting, or cleaning. Incontinence alone presents enough of a burden that social workers will help to find another placement for the sick person. Several social workers were emphatic about discouraging families from undertaking the care of an incontinent aged parent. Thus, professionals may interpret for the family members the conditions under which they may be relieved of any guilt about their relative's circumstances.

Strikingly, these working-class and lower middle-class families whom I interviewed managed to keep their ill and dying relatives *out* of the health care system. Few of these families ever came into contact with a social worker, and they had relatively limited exchange of information with other professionals. Hence, they were not alerted to the professionals' view of the cues that the patient's condition was presenting. Moreover, the justifications given to the family for placing their relative in a hospital or nursing home, and the mechanisms for accomplishing this, are not as available as when a family has access to professional consultation.

Unquestioned Obligations

The sense of obligation to provide a dying kinsman with care for as long as possible is a distinctive finding in our research. The supporting relatives' sense of obligation is *unquestioned* by them; shouldering the burden is the only viable alternative, and often is taken for granted as the only way of managing the situation.

In these circumstances, the relative takes on the problems, viewing them as his responsibility. Not to take on the burdens is conceived as *morally wrong*. In most cases of unquestioned obligation, the responsibility of the person giving care is simply understood and unstated. The understanding may consist of a shared viewpoint with the dying individual—most likely a husband or wife—which has existed over a number of years.

Hence, the surviving spouse may feel that not to do everything possible to keep the ill person out of the hospital, and especially out of the terminal wards, would constitute an unforgivable betrayal of trust. Consequently, super-human efforts are made to keep the patient at home. To illustrate, the wife may gradually transform the home into a micro-institution complete with a hospital bed, oxygen tank, hydraulic lift, and diet kitchen.

Underlying most cases of unquestioned obligation is the possibility or certainty of the kinsman's death. Time is a tremendously important aspect of how the burdens will be perceived and managed (Glaser and Strauss, 1968). The drama of certain death, particularly without warning, or early death increases the survivor's sense of *obligation*. In such instances we can suspect that individuals are reluctant to perceive their services to the dying as burdens.

An example of unquestioned obligation occurred when one young housewife had a long-standing agreement with her grandparents (who had raised her) that she would provide a home for whoever outlived the other; at the time her surviving grandfather came to live in the home, he himself had a prognosis of only three months to live. Knowing this, she attempted to make a special event out of grandpa's presence, and tried extra hard to make him happy. The children were solicitous and saw it as a novelty to make him a part of their home, despite the inconvenience and crowding he caused in their small house.

Compare the situation to one in which the time of death is uncertain. The novelty of the situation may soon or eventually be redefined as a nuisance. Fixing grandpa's lunch every day was fun at first, but the prospects of additional chores becoming part of a permanent routine are unlikely to be welcome. When the inconvenience of the oldster's presence becomes the most notable aspect of the situation, a definition of unquestioned obligation is unlikely to persist. If it is, it will have to be worked at, and its contradictions will have to be minimized. Despite the concern and original intent of the relatives, such arrangements tend to be fragile and difficult to maintain. Under the condition of the ill person's continued presence and uncertain death, he is more likely to become defined as a burden by the family, especially when brought into a nuclear family.

When relationships have been broken and death is certain, the relative is apt anyhow to feel obligated to make some attempt, however feeble, to make amends with the dying in order to place a shaky relationship in equilibrium before death finalizes the relationship. Under these circumstances, the extent of the potential burdening of the family is apt to be limited. In some cases, the burden may include taking the dying in, although it is more likely to mean visiting obligations. For example, a thirty-year-old son who hadn't spoken to his alcoholic father for eight years said, "Me and my father never talked for a long time. Then I heard the man had cancer—we talked." This was the limit for which the son would obligate himself. When an uncle put pressure on him to assume the funeral and burial costs, he refused. He implied that this type of responsibility should not be pushed on him, since after all, from his view, his father was to blame for his own situation. Any obligation beyond this was felt to be undeserved by the son. The relative merits of the dying person, in the eye of the potential helper, are likely to form the basis of the extent to which obligations are unquestioned by the helper.

Several women were aware that it was only their continued efforts that kept the oldster out of an institution for terminal cases. One Black woman who took in her grandfather when no one else wanted him made the following statement.

The nurses would say to me, "how did you take care of him so long?" I would say, I just loved him. I didn't want to see him in the hospital. I don't like those convalescent homes. They're in it for the money—they are kinda mean to them, too. I feel the same way about my uncle; I'm gonna keep him as long as I can.

Here, preventive home nursing care is used by the supporting relative as a way of intentionally delaying the time of final admission to a terminal care facility. In this instance it was the woman's negative view of institutions in addition to her attachment to her grandfather on which her feeling of obligation was based. Her perspective of the situation was unquestioned precisely *because* it was based on knowledge. Her assessment of institutional alternatives delimited her range of conceivable choices of how to handle her grandfather's care humanely.

Only when the situation becomes unbearable will the relative acknowledge the burden he is shouldering. Frequently the physical strains on the wife of a dying man result in the family physician's defining the care as a burden and directing changes. Until the point of unbearable strain, a wife may make concerted efforts to camouflage the fact that her husband is becoming a burden. Camouflaging can have several implications. First, it can serve as a way of refuting a wife's nagging suspicions that her husband is dying (Cf. Glaser and Strauss, 1965: Chapter 4). Second, with the realization that he is deteriorating, it can relieve her fears about the future after his death and keep her busy with many additional day-to-day tasks. Third, and perhaps most important, by camouflaging the burden, the wife is able to exert control on her husband's view of himself and help create a situation wherein he can die with dignity. In this way, she tacitly, or perhaps quite intentionally, helps to preserve her husband's self-image as a valuable man, as he progressively is able to do less. With this type of approach, his role in the family is reaffirmed even while he is dying.

Unsuspected Moribund Course

When the obligation is unquestioned, the relative is usually aware of the deterioration of the dying person, if not the actual dying itself. Clearly this is not always the case, and the death may come as something of a shock, even when the person was old or unwell. In the gradual aging pattern, deteriorating changes usually are not directly visible, and tend to be defined only through contrasts. This elusive quality sometimes make the changes strikingly apparent to those friends and family who rarely see the individual, while simultaneously the changes are unnoted by those who share everyday existence. In order for deterioration to be imperceptible, the relative must either be unaware of the burdens daily care imposes on him, or fail to make the connection between additional tasks, behavior changes and permanent deterioration.

Occasionally, those in closest contact will connect symptoms with prior incidents which were neither serious nor prolonged, if noted at all. This is especially likely when previous warnings concerning what to expect have not been provided by the medical profession. For an illustration of this, see the article about Richard Oakes, a noted Bay Area Indian leader (*San Francisco Chronicle,* 1970:3) who was badly beaten and did not receive care until hours later.

> Oakes lay unconscious and without medical attention for ten hours in his apartment in the San Francisco State College married students' housing area, according to his wife, Anne. Mrs. Oakes said she did not act sooner because she understood from the man who brought him home that he was just drunk. She realized his condition was serious at 8:15 a.m. when she noted his bloodied nose and black eye and was unable to awaken him.

Changes may not be perceived by the relative who is closest to the dying person when the latter already has reduced the amount of participation he contributes to various activities and when he exists in the same environment as the relative. When the dying person has confined himself for a period to his own home, and when the major changes have been so undramatic, it is less likely that others will catch small changes in daily ritual. Moreover, when shifts occur in the same setting, they are less apt to be noted by others, unless the present situation demands reevaluation of the past. A shifting scene dramatizes and illuminates the meaning of change of physical condition, especially so when the change in scene is the removal to a hospital or nursing home. The new scene may bring home the change more for the relative than a reappraisal of the patient's symptoms.

It is possible for relatives virtually to move in on the dying individual—as the amount of care is increased—*without* ever being explicitly aware that he is dying, or how much care they are giving him. For example, one woman was essentially doing everything for her mother just prior to her stroke, from keeping her clean to bringing in her food, although she never realized how her mother's health was rapidly failing. In this case, the cues are at least partially reconstructed after the physician discovers his findings and reveals them to the disbelieving family member, who then searches through the past to rediscover cues he had possibly overlooked. In part because the time and effort involved pose no particular problem to the assisting family member, cues signalling the deterioration remain undetected by them. As long as some semblance of the ordinary interaction between relatives is maintained, under the above conditions, the closest family member may not know what is happening. Furthermore, our data suggest that even after a first massive stroke, the relative who was closest but did not pick up the initial cues, undergoes considerable shock when death later occurs.

In the example above, the family member treated the situations as normal occurrences while she increased the services she provided for her mother (Cf. Davis, 1964:129). Any cues that she noted, she was subsequently able to normalize and this left her unsuspecting. The dying person himself sometimes normalizes the situation for the family and keeps them unaware of his condition. As long as he can maintain some semblance of independence in basic activities like eating, dressing, and toileting, he may preserve his prior status in the family. Moreover, by avoiding being a burden he disguises his moribund course.

Responsibility of Whom?

The individuals who take responsibility for care and decisions form an important variable in how burdens will be shouldered and for how long they will be supported. Clearly, in many instances, a spouse or child will become an advocate of home care and will seek to provide the patient with as much assistance as necessary. Here the assignment of the burden is *self-selective*, and other relatives may take this commitment by the supporting relative as justifying their own withdrawal from assuming responsibilities.

Not infrequently, however, self-selection occurs with simultaneous *assigning* of responsibilities by other family members. A repeated example of this occurs in the situation of one unmarried or divorced daughter who is considered to be more "available" by her siblings. She is seen as having fewer family obligations than those who are married and have children at home. Simultaneously, however, the woman self-selects herself on the basis of a more continuous and closer relationship with the ill person. In several cases, the self-selection extended to the point that the bond shared with the ill person had been the most significant one which the woman possessed.

Self-selection may also occur when a sympathetic relative perceives that no one else will act in behalf of the ill person, which would render him helpless and facing a long-term hospitalization. A self-selected supporting relative is most likely to intervene when the ill person is relatively alert and voices his own view (or despair) over his situation. Abandoning an articulate and aware patient to a prolonged institutionalized dying presents much more of a problem for the relatives than doing so to a person who is inarticulate or unaware of his actual circumstances of being a terminal case (Glaser and Strauss, 1965:Chapter 10). The patient's consciousness of the situation thus is a determinant in how he is viewed and what kind of arrangements can be made to accommodate him.

When the patient is aware of his plight and wishes to spend as much of his remaining time out of the hospital as possible, he may fight to preserve his independence and try to assume considerable responsibility for his own care. But, as time runs out, more tasks fall into the hands of the relative. As the dying trajectory proceeds, the supporting relative is apt to need back-up lines of assistance such as are provided by visiting nurses or other relatives. For example, a daughter may give all the daily care, and a son may visit every evening to help put grandmother back to bed. With increasing illness, the persons providing the back-up lines may find that they, too, are drawn into continuous work—most of their leisure hours becoming involved with adjunctive care of the dying individual. For example, two daughters who shouldered the care of their mother found that they were maintaining round-the-clock custodial nursing care complete with multiple daily bed changes, due to incontinence, special food preparation, and heavy lifting.

When the tasks become so arduous that the available individuals cannot handle them, the doctor is likely to try to relieve the family of the burdens of care by forcing them to make other arrangements. Or, frequently, the rate of deterioration proceeds so far that the family members acknowledge that the limits of their care have been over-extended, and begin to make other plans, if no dramatic change is caused by a sudden crisis like a heart attack or stroke.

Constructing Arrangements

As the older person shifts from a gradual-aging pattern of deterioration to a chronic-illness pattern with a dying trajectory, albeit slow, changes may become necessary in the kinds of living arrangements possible for him before hospitalization. Three general types of accommodations were found in our study. These include *independent living, old-age family living,* and *live-in nursing care.* An ill person may have all three types of situations before he reaches the final stages of dying, or may be hospitalized at any time that his deterioration increases.

Perhaps the most important property of all three types of arrangement is their relative tenuousness. Despite the interest and help of relatives, such arrangements are continually breaking down and the alternative for care which the family tried hardest to avoid may become their only choice. The numerous contingencies on which a plan rests are easily disrupted. Frequently, the main contingency of a planned arrangement is simply that the ill person does not get any worse. Then, as long as his condition remains status quo, other contingencies, such as the help provided him, remain stable and available. The prevailing definition may be "this much help, but no more;" then with a worsened condition, and the increased necessity of more help, resources for it become unavailable. Hence, within the context of a particular constructed arrangement, the assisting family member or members will tend to have a tolerance level for the amount of burdening that they can assume.

Independent Living. This is the type of arrangement for those living alone in their own domicile, typically when the pattern of deterioration is that of gradual aging. The arrangement may be scaled to the diminished needs and energy of the individual using it. Despite this, being able to maintain an independent existence, even of a limited kind, is often an important source of self-identification to the older person. Changing this arrangement may then become the point when the individual begins to feel despair. As one respondent described her grandfather,

> He never adjusted too well to the move, and I think it broke his spirit when he had to leave that house on 7th Street. He had his cronies—you know, all those guys would come over and drink beer and carry on, and play with the dog. Things were never the same for him after he had to move.

Tenacious independence is apt to be exhibited when the ill individual views other arrangements as untenable. Old people who value their independence and cling to it tenaciously sometimes are able to keep adjusting their daily existence so that they do not have to burden their family. Groceries are ordered and delivered; neighbors are asked for transportation to the doctor. Even though the costs include loneliness, inconvenience, and, not infrequently, health hazards, these individuals will attempt to carry on their usual routines and continue to assume the burden of self-care. This independent stance may have been a life-long tendency; however, it can also be based on the very accurate knowledge that the only two other possibilities are unwelcome—moving in with a relative or going to an institution.

Independent living may be constructed as a way of bringing an old person closer to the care and attention of a concerned relative. When arrangements are shifted, as the old person can do less, each shift may dramatically symbolize his decreasing participation in life and the additional burdens the family finds necessary to assume. Such changes may be programmed by the children so that their mother can maintain some independence and privacy as she grows older. Concurrently, *they* assume increasing responsibility for her care. As one widow grew older, her daughters arranged for her to move from her home 30 miles away to an apartment which was within walking distance of both daughters who helped her with groceries, laundry, and cleaning tasks. As the woman became increasingly ill, one daughter arranged for her to live in an adjoining apartment. Subsequently, this was followed by a shift to a shared apartment when she needed actual nursing care.

Old-Age Living. This is a type of family living where the aged or ill person lives or boards with another person such as a spouse, daughter or the entire family. The reason for the arrangement may be financial, although those involved expect the old person to enter a chronic-illness pattern of deterioration. The most tenuous arrangement is that which relies on the aged spouse as the supporting relative, since both partners are apt to have problems. Under these conditions, the ability to maintain an independent existence depends upon a delicate balance between what each person can do for himself and for the other person. Several social workers stated that this arrangement was generally unsatisfactory. These workers have found that neither person is able to assume the burdens imposed by the needs of the other, and as a consequence, deep hostilities between the aged couple often resulted.

As the aged couple become less independent, continuance of this mode of existence usually depends on the assistance of a younger person, particularly a daughter, but sometimes a housekeeper. In one case, both helped to assimilate the burdens of care; the housekeeper was full-time instead of live-in, so the daughter covered the nights and week-ends. When the burden of care is so great, coverage may be assisted by a visiting nurse.

Several families provided old-age living for persons who were not directly related to them, and a Black family took in a White retired friend, whose family ties were broken, for eight years. Usually, a family avoids boarders who, from the beginning, need sustained nursing care, and it is understood that a boarder will continue to help himself. When the family chooses a specific boarder, rather than feeling forced to accommodate him, the aged status of boarder may be allowed to shade into one of bona fide family member. If so, as he becomes ill, he may be given the solicitousness reserved only for closest relatives. This occurred when the White man boarded with the Black family. After his death, however, the woman acknowledged that his absence was not like missing one of her small family; it was like missing a grandfather.

Live-in Nursing Care. This type of living arrangement often is made when relatives realize that the older or ill person's health is degenerating into a chronic illness and dying pattern. The decision is often preceded by a bad fall, slight stroke or loss of the last arrangement because of money or complicating factors, e.g. stairs or a wheelchair. The decision to have the patient live-in may represent a last-ditch effort to keep him out of a nursing home.

When the family knowingly brings their relative home to give him nursing care, often they must integrate *their* routines into the round of care to be given him. This usually calls for mobilizing the help of others—family or nursing assistants. In several cases, the women of the family operated virtual nursing shifts by alternating their presence with the dying person with other obligations at work, their own families, and chores (like the daily trip to the laundromat). These efforts meant organizing all their nonworking hours in the service of the ill person.

As suggested earlier, wives are likely to attempt to undertake this kind of care. When care is given in the same surroundings, the fact of the seriousness or terminal state of the husband's illness may more easily be hidden from him (Glaser and Strauss, 1965: Chapter 5). Thus, enormous amounts of nursing care given at home may be given to terminal cancer patients whose doctors do not wish to disclose the diagnosis.

The pretense of the situation may be more of a burden on the wife than the strenuous care she is giving. Consider this woman's statement:

> The hardest thing was to know and keep it from him [dying]. Watch him slippin' away day by day. Then, he'd say things like, "Wonder why my food don't stay down?" and I'd have to say something like, "Well, my food don't always stay down either," and you'd have to be able to give a reason every time he said something like that, always have to have something to say when he said something.

Reevaluating the Burden

Direct changes in the constructed arrangements occur when ordered by a physician, who reevaluates the ongoing situation. These changes may serve to symbolize the person's condition and, significantly, herald his coming death. The changes in arrangements can be anticipated by the family. When the dying person has been recognizably ill for a prolonged period, usually several years, the family is apt to have projected the reevaluation of the situation into the future by discussing, and perhaps repeatedly rehearsing, the oncoming death and probable alternatives for themselves.

In contrast, not all families either are aware of the circumstances that they will eventually face, or choose to acknowledge these circumstances. As suggested above, when a certain amount of ambiguity exists and persists about the patient's status, the family may try to normalize the situation, or actively dis-attend to cues. Despite this, when there are common markers of participation—such as job, church, and community organizations—the kinsman's deterioration may not be so easily overlooked. Not only do the immediate family members note such changes, but even if they try to disavow them other people will remind them (Davis, 1964:123). For example, the son-in-law of a severely brain-damaged woman commented to her husband, "Poor thing, she doesn't remember very well, and she used to be so active." Even people who are almost strangers will give cues to the family which jar them into taking account of the changes. An unknown neighbor may say to the wife of a chronically ill man, "Your husband is getting worse, isn't he? I haven't seen him taking his walk these past few weeks." When the family is flooded with cues, they are likely to begin to reevaluate the situation. The combination of cues with increments in care can force the supporting relative into awareness of the probability of death. When this realization occurs, he may suddenly decide that he can no longer cope with the situation. At this point, he may seek professional prescriptions for a decision to relinquish his burden of care.

Keeping the Burden of Care at Home

When the dying individual is sentient, although virtually an invalid patient, he is in a position to negotiate over the arrangements provided for himself. In some cases, he can delay a medical order that he be sent to a nursing home. Though he may not be able to change *what* disposition is made, he is likely to influence *when* it occurs. Even in the situation where relatives had made plans over years to keep the patient at home for as long as possible, the decision to admit him to an institution was made after the medical decision had been made. The opposite tactic may be taken when the patient can negotiate himself. He may choose to enter a nursing home before it is even a possibility to his family.

The patient may adopt delaying tactics due to fear of being abandoned by the family. Hence, he may make every effort to be tenaciously independent and avoid making excessive demands upon his family, much less expose them to any feelings of despair which he might have. He is a model patient because he is afraid. When an aged parent fears being abandoned by an attentive son or daughter, and they respond to his fears, the chances are that the family will attempt to mobilize themselves in his behalf to the extent that a nursing home is constructed within the family's living quarters. In this situation the family cooperates with the stalling—usually when they assume that some improvement might occur or that death is imminent. Similarly, fear of abandonment by the ailing or dying spouse tends to tie the survivor in an almost inextricable bind to his burden of care. In contrast, when the marriage of the dying person is new, the spouse may pull out and force other relatives to shoulder the burden of care. This seems to be a common phenomenon with post-retirement marriage.

It is not uncommon for the physician to use his authority to reassure the dying person, and insist on the construction of a different arrangement to relieve the burdens on the spouse. The wife of one man who was extremely afraid reported:

He was upset by the move to the rest home, otherwise he accepted everything. He thought people were sent to a rest home when their family didn't want them no more. I tried to tell him, but he only really accepted it when the doctor talked to him. Dr. Staton said to me, "Look Norma, you couldn't handle it even if you had a nurse 24 hours a day, you couldn't do it. He needs equipment and special attention. Dr. Staton talked to him; he said, "If she keeps on doing it, she won't last." The doctor told him, "Arthur, your wife loves you. If you want to help, go to a rest home."

When stalling no longer works, or the patient himself cannot tolerate the toll that his stalling is taking on the family, he may attempt to manage his own situation through helping in the selection of a nursing home.

A more subtle consequence of a dying patient's alertness is that the family members usually feel compelled to take into account his realm of symbolic meanings. Knowing that he is alert obligates them to show respect for his preferences for alternatives. The importance which an aged or dying person attaches to his *home* may influence the amount of burden that his family will assume in order to keep him there. The extent that a given patient defines his situation as "home" has consequences for the kinds of dispositions that can be made for him.

When the family's definition of home coincides with the patient's, conditions are set so that no real consideration of other arrangements emerges until actually forced. Hence a definition of unquestioned obligation will prevail. Conversely, when the structure of the family is loose and fragmented, and the definition of "home" is also, the conditions develop for institutional placement being made more easily—any shift might result in this change.

When the old person is taken into a grown child's nuclear family, the likelihood of his being able to make a definition of "home" and have it stick becomes more difficult than when he exists in a somewhat separate environment. In subtle ways, the oldster is apt to feel that an encroachment on space and possessions represents something borrowed or lent. Old people who live in their own homes but have children join them, or essentially give their children furnishings for a house, are likely to settle in to a much greater degree, and, moreover, to remain at home. Furthermore, they feel the child *owes them* allegiance along with the willingness to assume the burdens of care. In short, the dying person has set up conditions wherein he attempts to force a definition of unquestioned obligation. In contrast, when an oldster is integrated into the family's daily round but not into the family structure, tacit understandings exist that he may make it his home as long as he does not become a burden.

When the boarder is not "at home," he is likely to maintain a certain distance from the person taking care of him, in addition to a stoical attitude about the necessity for the care. Furthermore, when the aged person does not define the arrangement as home, he is more likely to overlook the favors and assistance bestowed upon him by the people who take him in. In addition, he may not be attuned to their tolerance levels. Hence, when the time comes for evaluation of the burden of care, the family will probably opt for getting rid of him. In contrast, when the definition of home is not made by the boarder but the burdens become great, we can expect the situation will continue only when there are hidden benefits—such as occur when a woman cannot feed her own children without the additional money from the oldster's social security check, or when middle-class people expect an inheritance from him. Similarly, hidden commitments might serve to maintain such an arrangement, perhaps made as a promise to someone already deceased.

RELINQUISHING THE BURDEN

The Timing of Death and Changing Burdens

If the kinsman's deterioration is not interrupted by his sudden death at home, typically he will have to be admitted to a medical setting for the final stages of his dying. Albeit reluctantly, the supporting relative usually has to relinquish the burden of care.

At this juncture, the burdens involved dramatically shift. Although the relative is released from the enormous amount of work involved in care, new burdens develop, e.g., continued visiting. Ambiguity as to whether this *is* the final stage of dying may also pervade the situation. Thus, what at first may be regarded as a medical emergency—to keep the patient alive—may appear to develop into the last stages of his dying. The ambiguity of the time of death becomes part of the burden to be shouldered (Glaser and Strauss, 1965). This ambiguity may be cleared up by the patient's social death (Glaser and Strauss, 1968:61). For the family, his social death occurs when they see that the initial emergency has turned into a lingering dying. Consequently, the patient has essentially died at the point when the family's interest changes from hoping he can be pulled through to questioning, "Why don't they let him die?"

Here it is a case of social death occurring earlier than biological death. Hence, the symbolic meaning of the death for the relative occurs at a different and more inharmonious time than the actual death. Social death may occur gradually over time in cases of chronic disease. When this happens the actual death is not expected to be a shock, and the family may act as if the closest relative has lost his prerogative to express shock and profound grief. One daughter made the following remark at the time her father was dying. "She [the mother] should accept it—after all she has watched him die for two years." Carrying this thinking further, when people who have been ill for years finally enter the dying trajectory, they may have been so excluded and estranged from the usual family interaction and ongoing events that they have lost meaning as a *person* to the rest of the group; so death is somewhat anti-climactic.

Social death may also occur at the point when the housekeeping arrangements are drastically changed. The most pointed example of this was when a grandmother was placed in a nursing home and was never again spoken of or visited. A similar situation was reported by a nurse working on the terminal wards of a county institution. When she called a female patient's son to request permission to cut her hair, his response was, "Goodness, is she still alive?"

More often, the relative will attempt to reconstruct the past in order to point to a time when logically their kinsman ceased to exist as the individual known in the past. "She died at the point when her heart stopped at Stanford." The social death is confirmed when the hospital staff announces that no more can be done, and that the family will have to make other arrangements.

Whether or not the family defines social death as occurring, the continued presence of the patient places certain burdens upon the family, not the least of which is their observation that the dying person is suffering. Obligations to him have to be weighed against the need to preserve the energies of the closest relatives. These dilemmas over what to do are confronted by anguished family members. Since she doesn't want him to die alone, should the wife of a dying man remain at his bedside for what might turn out to be many days? Or, should she follow the advice of the physician who encourages her to begin to get back to her usual routines and wait and see?

The disruption of the life of the family members, and the burdens which it places upon them, emerge even when the most optimum conditions have been constructed. One man tried to view his extremely brain-damaged wife as dead, and build a new life for himself since she would never be able to come home. However, his wife was placed in a nursing home five minutes away from the family business. Although his visits were decreased, he was not completely able to make the shift. The dilemma was written all over the man's face. Intellectually he knew he *should* construct a new life without her. However, it was impossible for him to manage this, psychologically and socially. The phone calls about "How's Sue?" (his wife) were so numerous that for a period he refused to answer the phone. Also, other reminders tied him to the past—not the least was the woman's recognition of, and attachment to, him. Whenever anyone else visited, her first and repeated question was "Where's Daddy?" This man was so torn by the situation that he would not arrange for an attending physician to supervise her case at the nursing home. When told that the staff had to be able to notify a doctor "in case of an emergency," he said, "That's exactly what we don't want. When her pulse goes down, they'll just pull her through again, and what's it all for? It makes everyone suffer. She died months ago."

In this case the husband was not able to treat his wife as "socially dead," under the condition that her living arrangement was so close and she frequently recognizes him. If, on the other hand, she became permanently comatose, then he could reconcile himself to her death and maintain his self-respect while he attempted to construct another life. Analytically, the interesting aspect of such a case is that the husband was trying to define the situation as a social death, with the support of sympathetic professionals, but that the two conditions of his wife's situation—proximity and recognition of family—invalidated this definition and simultaneously served to increase the emotional burdens which the family now shouldered.

Attachment to the Burden

In the anecdote above, treating the situation as a social death was attempted *before* biological death. In other cases, the supporting relative may attempt to keep the deceased socially alive beyond the point of actual death. Under these circumstances, the attachment of the supporting relative for the patient extends beyond the shared relationship they had together to the style of existence including the daily routine of physical care and housekeeping. When this occurs, the supporting relative may attempt to follow the routines to which she has become attached even though they are no longer necessary. Several of the middle-aged women who took care of their aged mothers were suddenly released. Without the burdens of care, they felt they were not really contributing anything of meaning to others. In contrast to the devotion and services they had previously provided, being free to pursue their own interests appeared inconsequential. Perhaps without quite realizing it, assuming the burden of care had become the major source of personal fulfillment for these women.

When so much of the supporting relative's self is invested in the patient and his care, relinquishing both becomes problematic, if not traumatic. The relative is tied to the past. One wife said, "I don't even feel it—no changes. I can still see myself getting ready to go to the hospital. I can't accept it that he is gone." When a friend suggested to another new widow that she pursue some prior interests, she retorted, "Why should I do that? Everything I had in life that meant something to me is gone now." When the closest relative's life is so inextricably intertwined with the dying person, the death is more likely to be a shock. This was so with women who gave burdensome care but did not realize the extent of their undertakings until it was relinquished. For them the burden was more than unquestioned, it was unrealized.

CONCLUSION

Since most older people live in non-institutionalized settings, the problems of the burdens of care of the dying confront most families, for at least a period of time, if not up until the final stages of dying. The closer the kinship relatedness, attachment, and proximity, the more likely the burden of care will be assumed by the family. If these conditions exist and the supporting relative is aware of the ill person's deterioration, then the family may maintain a definition of unquestioned obligation for the burden of care.

Clearly, taking on the burden of care is an important part of family existence for a number of these cases. The professionals they dealt with were described as more equipped to help them relinquish the burden than able to offer concrete alternatives for managing it more easily at home. The awareness of professionals of the structural conditions which surround individual situations may give them helpful guidelines for recommending assisting measures that can be used to compensate for the changing circumstances in home care.

REFERENCES

Davis, F. *Passage through crisis*. Indianapolis: Bobbs-Merrill, 1963.
——— Deviance disavowal: The management of strained interaction by the visibly handicapped. In H.S. Becker (Ed.) *The other side*. Glencoe: The Free Press, 1964, 119-138.
Glaser, B. G., & Strauss, A. L. *Awareness of dying*. Chicago: Aldine, 1965.
——— *Time for dying*. Chicago: Aldine, 1968.
San Francisco Chronicle, Indian leader is badly beaten (June 13, 1970), 3.
Strauss, A. L., & Glaser, B. G. *Anguish*. Mill Valley, Calif.: Sociology Press, 1970.
Sudnow, D. *Passing on*. Englewood Cliffs, N.J.: Prentice-Hall, 1967.

CHAPTER
8

A Psychosocial Aspect
of Terminal Care:
Anticipatory Grief[1]

Robert Fulton and Julie Fulton

Death in contemporary society is increasingly an experience of the aged. Of the 2 million persons who will die in the United States this year, almost two-thirds of them (62 percent) will be 65 years of age or over, although this age group represents only 9 percent of the total population. Children under the age of 15, on the other hand, account for 29 percent of the total United States population but only 5.5 percent of the total deaths.[2] This is in sharp contrast to the mortality statistics in 1900, for instance, when proportionally, far more children died. At that time, children under the age of 15 accounted for 34 percent of the population—approximately the same proportion as today—but this age group accounted for 53 percent of the total deaths. In the same year, persons age 65 and over accounted for 4 percent of the total population, and 17 percent of all deaths.[3] These changes in mortality statistics are further reflected in life-expectancy figures. A person born in 1900 had a life-expectancy of 47.3 years, whereas a person born in 1967 could expect to live 70.5 years.[4]

The context in which dying and death are experienced in the United States has also undergone a significant change. Of the two million deaths estimated for 1970, almost two-thirds (64 percent) will take place outside the home in either a hospital or a nursing home.[5] The number of persons who will go to such a setting eventually to die can be expected to increase with the prospect of Medicare, more sophisticated medical technology, and the progressive segregation of the aged from families. Medical science, with its associated public health programs, has reduced the mortality rate and prolonged the life-expectancy of millions of our citizens. The extension and bureaucratization of medical health services, therefore, not only has changed the age at which a person can expect to die, but, in addition, has changed the time and place of his death.

---

[1] Prepared for the symposium, *Psychosocial Aspects of Terminal Care,* Columbia University, November 6 and 7, 1970.
[2] National Center for Health Statistics, *Monthly Vital Statistics Report,* Provisional Statistics, Annual Summary for the United States, 1968, Vol. 17, No. 3 (August 15, 1969) Washington, D. C., Table 6, p. 16; and U.S. Department of Commerce, Bureau of the Census, *Population Estimates: July 1, 1968,* p. 25, No. 400, (August 13, 1968), Table 2, p. 2.
[3] U.S. Department of Commerce, U.S. Bureau of the Census, *Special Report: Mortality Statistics 1900-04.* (Washington, D. C., Government Printing Office, 1906), Table 2, p. 22; and U.S. Bureau of the Census, *Historical Statistics of the United States, Colonial Times to 1957,* a Statistical Abstract Supplement, Washington, D.C., 1960, Table: Series A 71-85, p.10.
[4] U.S. Bureau of the Census, *Historical Statistics of the United States, Colonial Times to 1957,* a Statistical Abstract Supplement, Washington, D.C., 1960, Table: Series B 92-100, p. 25; and U.S. Bureau of Census, *Statistical Abstracts of the United States: 1970* (91st edition), Washington, D.C., 1970, Table 65, p.53.
[5] This statement is based upon the fact that the trend is toward greater hospitalization and institutionalization of the chronically ill and dying patient. The data for 1960 show that 60% of all deaths occurred in hospitals or institutions. See *Vital Statistics of the United States,* 1958, Vol. II, Table 67, Public Health Service, Washington, D.C., U.S. Government Printing Office, 1960.

The place to which the elderly go to die has recently drawn the attention of medical and social science investigators. Glaser and Strauss (1965, 1968) have studied the interaction between hospital staffs and chronically ill and dying patients. Quint (1967) has explored the occupational problems that dying and death present the student nurse. Sudnow (1967) has focused his research on the manner of treatment accorded dying and dead patients in a public, as opposed to a private, hospital, while Kübler-Ross (1969) has interviewed the dying patient in an attempt to understand more fully the many issues and questions that he must confront with the prospect of imminent death.

These and other investigators have directed their attention to the experience of the dying patient and the major problems he presents the institution and the staff responsible for his care. Little attention, however, has been paid to his survivors. Blauner (1966), giving a possible reason for this, points out that the reversal in mortality statistics over the past few decades has given dying and death a different meaning for the survivors. The change in mortality statistics has directly affected family relations. Blauner observes that the death of an elderly person today need not touch the emotional life of his family nor the social life of a community to the same degree that it once might have. The elderly in contemporary society are increasingly retired from gainful employment and other social activities, and they are frequently less central to the lives of their families than were the elderly in the past. The greater life-expectancy today, and the sense of having lived out one's life in full, permit the dying person, as well as his survivors, to accept his death more readily. With the sudden death of a young child or of a husband or wife in the middle years, there is a sense of the deceased having been cheated out of life and of the survivors having suffered a great loss. In contrast to this reaction, Blauner feels that the quality of a person's death in an institutional setting, particularly the death of an elderly person, does not evoke the same kinds of responses that we have traditionally expected of the bereaved. Medical technology not only makes possible the prolongation of life, it is also the basis for repeated and often extended separations of the chronically ill or dying person from his family. Such separations reduce familial and friendship contacts and also serve to weaken social and emotional commitments. The disengagement of the aged from their families prior to their death, therefore, means that their death will little affect the life of the family. As Blauner (1966) has observed, the death of an important social leader, such as President Kennedy, can seriously disrupt the equilibrium of a modern community. The death of the elderly, on the other hand, less relevant as they are to the life of their families and to the functioning of modern society, does not cause such a rupture.

This is not to say that there is no grief felt at the loss of an elderly parent or relative. Rather it is to point out that the degree or intensity of one's grief at the time of the death is a function of the kind of death experienced. A distinction must be made, in other words, between what can be termed a "high-grief-potential" death and a "low-grief-potential" death. A high-grief-potential death can be occasioned by the sudden accidental death of a man or woman upon whom others depend for their physical and/or psychological well-being. Such a death usually will precipitate a series of intense reactions, which Erich Lindemann (1944) has characterized as "normal grief."

According to Lindemann, normal grief can give rise to such symptoms as sensations of somatic distress, choking with shortness of breath, a need for sighing, an empty feeling in the abdomen, a feeling of tightness in the throat, lack of muscular power, and intense distress described as tension or mental pain. In addition to these somatic reactions,

Lindemann noted that the bereaved must contend with other grief related symptoms. The bereaved person will evince a preoccupation with the image of the deceased. He will also feel guilt, and in certain instances, show extreme hostility. Moreover, he may be unable to execute his normal patterns of conduct. The duration of the grief reaction depends upon the success with which a person does what Lindemann refers to as the "grief work"—emancipating himself from his emotional bondage to the deceased and developing new emotional attachments.

When grief symptoms are seemingly absent, on the other hand, it may mean one of two things: either the survivor is suppressing his feelings of intense grief—which is an important but separate issue in and of itself—or, the death did not evoke the emotional reactions Lindemann (1944) has described. A death in which these reactions are indeed absent and are not merely suppressed is a low-grief-potential death. For many people today, the death of an elderly relative occasions only the barest acknowledgement, and such a death might properly be designated as a "low-grief" death. There are many factors which might generate such a response, but one of the most important, we believe, is the phenomenon of "anticipatory grief."

The remainder of this chapter, then, will be a discussion of anticipatory grief, and the reasons for both its increasing presence and increasing importance in contemporary society.

As has been pointed out, the death that a family experiences today is most frequently the death of one of its elderly members. Moreover, prior to his death, the elderly member may have been removed from the inner family circle. He may have spent several periods in a hospital or a nursing home prior to his admission to a terminal hospital. In any event, his family has experienced periods of separation from him due to his incapacity or illness. The low-grief response expressed by family members at the time of his death may be due to what has been termed by Lindemann (1944) as anticipatory grief. That is, the family members are so concerned with their adjustment in the face of the potential loss that they slowly experience all the phases of normal grief as they cope with the illness or endure the separation prior to the death. Over an extended period of time, therefore, the family members may (1) experience depression, (2) feel a heightened concern for the ill member, (3) rehearse his death, and (4) attempt to adjust to the various consequences of it. By the time the death occurs the family will, to the extent that they have anticipated the death or dissipated their grief, display little or no emotion.

ANTICIPATORY GRIEF

Anticipatory grief is not a recent psychic phenomenon, nor is it necessarily associated only with death. Both Lindemann (1944) and Rosenbaum (1944) have found what they would describe as genuine grief reactions in persons who had experienced separation due to the demands of military duty. Lindemann cites the case of a soldier recently returned from combat who complained that his wife no longer loved him and that she was seeking a divorce. It was Lindemann's opinion, following a review of the facts in the case, that the soldier's wife had so effectively worked through her grief over his separation and possible death that, emotionally, she had completely emancipated herself from her husband. While this reaction may well form a safeguard against the impact of the eventuality of death or a permanent separation, it is apparent that it has important as well as unforeseen consequences for survivors. It has been found, for instance, that a great many of those who are released from military service, from jail, or from hospitals cannot be reintegrated into their families; in their absence, their families have established new role relationships which no longer include them. It may well be, for instance, that a significant variable in the poor adjustment of men released from prison, as suggested by their high rate of recidivism, is the fact that their significant others are no longer emotionally capable of incorporating them into the family or friendship circle; they are incapable of giving them the kind of emotional support they need to make a satisfactory readjustment to the outside world (see Glaser, 1964, for a fuller discussion of recidivism).

In each of the examples of anticipatory grief, family members have worked through their grief without a death actually having occurred. Appropriate responses and outward expressions of one's emotions in instances of this sort are at best vague and ill-defined. That is, in our society, it is considered appropriate either to laugh or to cry—or even to behave casually—when greeting a returning serviceman or someone who has been separated for a long time from the family. The only inappropriate response would be to show a lack of pleasure at this return. At death, however, there is a cultural directive for the bereaved to mourn. Joyful, casual, or business-as-usual behavior is considered both inappropriate and disrespectful.

Culturally, as Volkart (1957) has pointed out, we tend to perceive the death of a person as a loss, particularly the death of a close family member. Moreover, we expect the survivors as bereaved individuals to show grief. We expect this because culturally we feel it is natural, proper, and desirable: natural to grieve, proper to show respect, and desirable to purge ourselves of the grief. The question of whether grieving is internally motivated or externally induced is generally not an issue with us. We assume that any observed behavior and the feelings that we impute to that behavior express the relationship between the deceased and his survivors. Regardless of the actual relationship that might have existed prior to the death, we tend to idealize the relationship once death has occurred, and to expect expressions of normal grief.

This is an expectation held not only by the average man, but it is held also by members of the medical profession. They have accepted and internalized these conventional categories of thought long before they became nurses or doctors. There is growing evidence that medical personnel who have attended the deceased patient are highly critical of his family members and friends whose behavior appears to be inappropriate, incongruous, or callous; they are responding negatively to family members who display such seeming disregard for their dead relatives.[6] To the extent, however, that such behavior is due to anticipatory grief, it is important for medical personnel and other social caretakers to temper their reactions and withhold their judgment of the survivors. To respond angrily, or in any other way show disapproval of the behavior of the

---

[6] At a recent symposium on the terminal care of the dying, a hospital staff member expressed strong objections to what she described as the callous behavior of family members upon the death of an elderly relative. She found their behavior so characteristically indifferent to the deceased, particularly at the funeral, that she publicly called for their exclusion from the funeral. Moreover, she proposed that the funeral itself should be conducted from the hospital in order to allow for attendance of the hospital staff members, who according to her, were usually more concerned over the death of one of their patients than was the bereaved family.

This observation has been increasingly echoed in comments directed to the senior author by nurses and hospital staff members as well as by nursing home attendants and funeral directors over the past few years.

survivors, is to act in a lay rather than a professional manner, possibly aggravating an already troubled situation. What must be appreciated here is that the survivors themselves can be just as surprised and just as disturbed by their lack of response at the death of a close relative or friend as are the medical personnel. The absence of any feeling for the death can be very disturbing to the bereaved, and in the face of the cultural directive to mourn, can be conducive to a sense of guilt or a feeling of shame.

Lifton (1963) documents a similar guilt reaction in his study of the survivors of the atomic bomb in Hiroshima. In recounting the life history of the *hibakusha*, as the Hiroshima survivors are called, a significant aspect of their psychological reaction to the horror and chaos that they experienced was a closing-off of their capacity to feel or to respond to the condition of others. While, as Lifton points out—and it is a point to be stressed—psychological closure permitted the survivors to function in the situation and to do what they could for themselves as well as for the injured and dying, it was, Lifton believes, nevertheless an element in the shame and guilt that swept over these survivors afterwards. Their failure to respond to an event as profoundly tragic as Hiroshima was for them a mystifying as well as a demoralizing experience. How could anyone continue to live, eat, and sleep in the face of such a cataclysm? How could anyone go about the daily task of disposing of corpses, comforting the dying, or rendering assistance to the injured without shedding a tear? The psychological closure that Lifton discusses in his essay appears to mirror the protective function of anticipatory grief, as well as to reflect its similar consequences. That is, the *hibakusha* were unable to feel any grief at the time it was expected of them, and in reflecting upon this, they suffered an extreme sense of guilt. In situations in which grieving is considered appropriate, we not only expect it of others, but they also expect it of themselves. The *hibakusha* responded with guilt and shame at having gone through the death experiences of others with little or no feeling.

One of the unanticipated consequences of anticipatory grief, therefore, is the undeserved critical judgment by others, as well as the critical judgment of one's self.

That such psychological factors are at work is illustrated in the research of Natterson and Knudson (1960) in which the responses of 33 mothers of fatally ill children were studied. They reported:

> Initially, most mothers (25 of 33) were tense, anxious, withdrawn and readily inclined to weep. They reacted in a disbelieving manner, tending to deny either the diagnosis of the disease or its fatal outcome. They wanted to be with their children as much as possible, often tending to cling to them physically. This staying with the child was sometimes without much regard for the needs of the remainder of the family. Hope for the child was stressed, but in a nonspecific way—"Something will be discovered." They wanted, often in an irrational manner, to try anything in the way of new treatment that might offer hope for a cure (p 459).

After a period of more than four months, 16 out of 19 mothers whose children subsequently died showed calm acceptance of the child's anticipated death. As Natterson and Knudson describe it:

> These mothers gradually became less tense and anxious. They stopped denying the diagnosis or its prognosis. Their hope for the child became more specific, often related to particular scientific efforts. A considerable interest in the investigative program often developed at this time. There was a tendency to see the medical problem in its broader aspects, with the beginning of an expressed desire to help all children. Mothers during this period tended to cling less to their own children, encouraging them to participate in school or occupational therapy activities. They often helped in the care of other children on the ward and were generally more social. They spoke

more about fulfilling family obligations. In most instances, this reaction gradually gave rise to a calm terminal reaction . . . (p 460).

While Natterson and Knudson chose to describe the change in the mother's attitude as one of "sublimation," we are prone to suggest that what they observed among the mothers was anticipatory grief.

In sharp contrast to the mother's behavior was the behavior observed among almost all staff members. Initially the staff members' reactions to a particular child were not marked. But, as the staff became increasingly involved in the child's problem, they were prone not only to exert themselves more on the child's behalf but also were reluctant to forego any program of medication that might prolong the child's life. Upon the death, it was noted that the staff became depressive, guilty, and self-examining. Such a disparate reaction between the mothers and the staff is potentially fraught with difficulties. Not only were they out of phase in their response to the death of the child, but also the emotional response of the medical staff in the terminal stage of the dying could well serve to generate a sense of shame or guilt in the mothers who had worked through their grief. The inability of the medical staff, moreover, to remain dispassionate in the face of what is readily recognized as a tragic death, threatened not only to interfere with their medical judgment regarding reasonable measures in the situation, but also served as a marker of appropriate behavior for the mothers and invited a sense of shame or guilt among those who could not generate comparable feelings.

In a retrospective study of 20 families whose children died of leukemia, Binger et al. (1969) confirm the anticipatory grief reaction of the parents as reported by Natterson and Knudson. However, the reaction of some of the physicians they observed to the child's death was opposite to the reaction observed by Natterson and Knudson. They write:

> The professional has his own problems in coping with the imminent death of a child. He is distressed and often feels guilty about the failure of therapy. Simultaneously he is troubled by his own fears and anxieties about death and feels inadequate to support the dying child and his parents. Faced with these conflicts he often avoids the patient or family or makes himself unapproachable by presenting a facade of busyness, impatience, or formality. Thus at a time when most needed, the professional often assumes a neutral or even negative role in contacts with the family of the dying child (p 415).

It was reported by these researchers that more than a quarter of the families believed that the physician and staff members became more remote as the child's condition worsened. Not only was the child physically more isolated (a precaution taken because of leukopenia and the chance of infection) but he was actively "avoided" by the staff as well.

It should be noted that the origin of the physicians' responses in the Natterson and Knudson study as well as in the Binger study were in fact the same. Both studies report feelings of inadequacy, guilt, and anxiety among the physicians at not being able to keep the child alive. The differing manner in which the physicians chose to respond to these similar feelings points up the lack of appropriate behavioral norms for physicians in the face of death.

Binger et al. conclude that when professional personnel understand the attitudes of the parents and are prepared to respond to their needs, they will become a valuable source of help to the family *instead* of getting caught up in a situation laden with mutual hostility and recriminations.

Another finding of the Binger study underscores the need for medical personnel to understand the dynamics of grief in order to assist families in such circumstances. The researchers found that in 11 of the 20 families, one or more members had emotional disturbances severe enough to require psychiatric guidance. None, they report, had required such help before. The emotional disturbances included:

> several cases of severe depression requiring admission to a psychiatric hospital, a conversion reaction wherein a man was temporarily unable to talk, severe psychoneurotic symptoms and behavioral changes in siblings. In some of the other families milder disturbances were also reported in both the adults and the children (p 417).

It is the conclusion of Binger and his colleagues that supportive therapy and counseling for parents and siblings should be considered an essential aspect of total care so that such untoward reactions to death as these can be both understood and prevented in the future.

But perhaps the most significant implication that anticipatory grief has, is for the dying patient himself. While he, along with his survivors, must come to *accept* his illness and his death, it is a problematical thing for him to know whether his survivors are in fact concerned or grieved at his dying. While the answer to this question can only be found within the context of a specific case, there are indications that suggest that this question will loom larger as more and more elderly people, in particular, are removed to nursing homes or terminal hospitals. While conclusive evidence is lacking at this time a number of observers have noted that the visits of family members to chronically ill or dying patients in hospitals or nursing homes diminish in frequency and length soon after their relative is placed in the institution. Riley and Foner (1968) report, moreover, on the basis of different studies, that a disproportionate number of deaths occur among elderly patients soon after commitment to an institution. While it is, of course, possible that the timing of placements in institutions may be due to the severity of the illness of the patient, nonetheless it is also possible—and deserves more careful study—that the precipitous rise in patients' deaths immediately following their commitment to the institution may be a response to their removal from their own homes. Leiberman (1961), for example, reports that death rates among residents in an old-age home during the first year after admission were more than twice as high as for the same population while it was on the waiting list. He concluded, moreover, that early mortality did not appear to be clearly associated either with poor physical health or with age at first admission. Such a finding suggests that still unexplored factors may account for this phenomenon.

In the case of the leukemia victims, we have seen that two grief trajectories can operate in the situation of the institutionalized dying patient: as the family comes to accept the death, their emotional involvement diminishes or becomes intellectualized and diffuse, whereas the medical staff may become caught up in the drama of the death and their emotional investment in the patient may increase (Natterson & Knudson, 1960). The turning away of family members at this time, in a psychological as well as a physical sense, can create an insurmountable problem for the patient. At a time when he needs the support, comfort, and reassurance of his family, the phenomenon of anticipatory grief can serve to block such support. The absence of tears or expressions of concern may compel the patient to grieve not only for his own death, but also for the seeming loss of his family's love.

In response to the difficult problems inherent in this situation, several different medical centers are sponsoring programs in grief therapy with the hope that para-medical personnel might play a supportive role as surrogate relatives. While this well-intentioned effort is prompted by the highest ideals of medicine and social service, its consequence may be to aggravate an already difficult situation. It seems to us that the professional functionary could play a more valuable role, once he himself understands the dynamics of anticipatory grief, by explaining and interpreting the phenomenon to the patient, as well as to his relatives and friends. The patient would be better served if his relatives and friends were to be drawn back into an enlightened relationship with him rather than, as it appears to be proposed, that they be replaced by well-meaning but nevertheless professional sympathizers.

It should be quite apparent that the task of dying is not simply a polite exchange of confidences or an expression of affection or concern. Dying involves the taking of one's leave from all of those who have been important to the one who is about to die. The array of questions and issues dealing with such disparate concerns as: the education of a grandchild, the marriage of a daughter or niece, the disposition of a ring to a favorite cousin—to say nothing of how old friendships and animosities are to be concluded—can only be the business of the dying patient and those members of his family or friendship group that are immediately and directly involved. To propose a program of professional intervention for more than those patients who are completely without relatives or friends is, in the face of the total number of dying, to assume what would eventually be an impossible task, as well as one which ultimately would defeat its own purpose.

Finally, the effects of anticipatory grief are felt again when the family confronts the funeral. Traditionally, the funeral has served not only as a ceremony to dispose of the dead, but also it has been recognized as a supportive and integrative ceremony which aids the bereaved to reorient themselves from the shock of death (see Mandelbaum, 1959; Malinowski, 1938). The funeral, moreover, has had other functions, which, while not readily perceived or understood, are nevertheless important (see Fulton, 1971). For instance, reciprocal social obligations are often reinacted and reinforced in the course of a funeral. In this way, the role of a participant not only reflects his position in the community but the community structure itself is also reaffirmed. Moreover, funerary expectations pertaining to dress, demeanor, and social intercourse both declare and reconfirm family cohesion. The family and the larger kinship system are also acknowledged at the time of a death. Distant family members, moreover, are not only expected to console the immediate survivors, but may also share in the expenses of the funeral. Through the participation in a funeral, an individual is presented with and reminded of the various parts and personnel of his social world. The visitation or wake, the funeral service, the interrment or disposal service, and finally the concluding family meal all serve to invoke a sense of being part of a larger social whole, just as the observed order of precedence in this rite of passage reminds one that there is structure and order in the social system.

The death of a person today, however, is perceived by some as simply a matter of disposal. As Blauner (1966) has pointed out, the role of the elderly in contemporary society no longer necessitates a funeral for them such as we have just described. The decline in religious beliefs, moreover, and the strong impetus toward worth (associated or identified with one's contribution to society), have merely added to this trend.

We would argue that the phenomenon of anticipatory grief is also an important variable in this development. A survivor who is emotionally emancipated from a deceased individual will not necessarily feel that the traditional funeral rite is an appropriate response to the death. Rather, he may well believe that the expeditious disposal of the body is most in keeping with the prior reduced status of the decreased, as well as with his own feelings and desires. Anticipatory grief in this context may have positive consequences for the survivor. He has anticipatorily accepted the death and is able to function in his new social environment without the deceased present. To the extent that this is so, he is tempted to dismiss those things associated with the funeral which historically have served as a religious or social aid to his understanding of the death, as well as an aid to his adjustment to it. But, as we have tried to suggest, the funeral offers somewhat more than that. The funeral, like other rituals, ceremonies, rites of passage, pageants, and festivals, serves to reinforce a sense of community as it fashions and refashions social bonds. A recent national study (conducted by the senior author) concerning contemporary funeral practices shows that in certain areas of the country, particularly on the East and West coasts, there is a tendency for families to modify traditional funeral rites to the point where no one except the immediate members of the family are present. In addition, there is a tendency with such privatizations of the funeral, to modify mortuary rites to the barest requirements including, in some instances, the elimination of the public death notice itself. While it is probably not true that the traditional funeral will wither away in contemporary America, as Blauner suggests, there is indeed evidence to suggest that for great numbers of people it will be significantly different from what it has been.

It is our contention that the phenomenon of anticipatory grief serves to play a large part in this transition, inasmuch as it allows the survivors to make new and different decisions about the disposal of their dead. Although the phenomenon of anticipatory grief can be functional for the adjustment of the immediately bereaved, it may, as we have pointed out, be dysfunctional for the dying patient as well as for the extended social group. In the case of the privatized funeral, for example, another set of behaviors is attenuated—a set of behaviors which have served historically to maintain and enhance familial, friendship, and community relationships. The failure to acknowledge a death publicly not only has humanistic implications for our identity and worth as human beings, and political implications for our status as citizens, such a failure also closes off still another avenue where sympathy, love, and affection may be given and received.

CONCLUSION

As a psychological phenomenon with social consequences, anticipatory grief, as we have tried to show, confronts us with a two-edged effect. It possesses the capacity to enhance our lives and secure our well-being, while possessing at the same time the power to undermine our fragile existence and rupture our tenuous social bonds.

It has been the intention of this chapter to point out these implications of anticipatory grief so that we may better understand its functioning. In doing so, we may succeed in turning it to our account rather than to suffer its consequences through our ignorance or misapprehension of its role in our lives.

REFERENCES

Binger, C. M., Ablin, A. R., Feurstein, R. C., Kushner, J. H., Zoger, S., & Mikkelsen, C. Childhood leukemia: Emotional impact on patient and family. *New England Journal of Medicine*, 1969, 280, 414-418.

Blauner, R. Death and social structure. *Psychiatry,* 1966, 25, 378-394.
Fulton, R. Contemporary funeral practices. In H. C. Raether (Ed.), *Modern funeral service.* New York: Prentice-Hall, 1971.
Glaser, D. *The effectiveness of a prison and parole system.* Indianopolis: Bobbs-Merrill Co., 1964.
Glaser, B., & Strauss, A. *Awareness of dying.* Chicago: Aldine Press, 1965.
———*Time for dying.* Chicago: Aldine Press, 1968.
Kübler-Ross, E. *On death and dying.* London: Collier-Macmillan, 1969.
Liebermann, M. A. The relationship of mortality rates to entrance to a home for the aged. *Geriatrics,* 1961, 16, 515-519.
Lifton, R. J. Psychological effects of the atomic bomb in Hiroshima: The theme of death. *Daedalus,* 1963, 92, 462-497.
Lindemann, E. Symptomatology and management of acute grief. *American Journal of Psychiatry,* 1944, 101, 141-148.
Malinowski, B. *Magic, science, and religion and other essays.* Boston: Beacon Press, 1938.
Mandelbaum, D. G. Social uses of funeral rites. In H. Feifel (Ed.), *The meaning of death.* New York: McGraw-Hill, 1959.
Natterson, J. M., & Knudson, A. G. Observations concerning fear of death in fatally ill children and their mothers. *Psychosomatic Medicine,* 1960, 22, 456-463.
Quint, J. *The nurse and the dying patient.* New York: Macmillan Co., 1967.
Riley, M., & Foner, A. *Aging and society.* New York: Russell Sage Foundation, 1968.
Rosenbaum, M. Emotional aspects of wartime separation. *Family,* 1944, 24, 337-341.
Sudnow, D. *Passing on.* Englewood Cliffs, New Jersey: Prentice-Hall, 1967.
Volkart, E. H., with Michael, S. T. Bereavement and mental health. In A. H. Leighton, J. A. Clausen, & R. N. Wilson (Eds.), *Explorations in social psychiatry.* New York: Basic Books, 1957.

CHAPTER
9

The Reactions of Family Systems to Sudden and Unexpected Death[1,2]

Rita R. Vollman, Amy Ganzert, Lewis Picher, and W. Vail Williams

This chapter describes a portion of the clinical material gathered from the first year of a four-year research grant,[2] studying the application of crisis intervention techniques to bereaved families as a means of primary prevention. The hypothesis of this study is that intervention at the time of a sudden death will reduce the higher morbidity and mortality rates found by other workers (e.g., Rees and Lutkins, 1967) to occur in the surviving family members.

The focus of the present chapter is to discuss some of the concepts that have evolved during our work with bereaved families. These concepts have given us a line of vision which makes clear the kinds of aid that can be offered and accepted, and that will, hopefully, prevent further disorganization in these families which are already in crisis. Specifically, the study centers around the interactive patterns between the family and society, which determine whether or not the family is open to intervention, and the variables operating within the family itself that affect the immediate reaction to the death as well as its eventual reorganization.

Our main working assumption is that families are more than the composite blood or marriage related group that can be counted in fixed terms. Rather, we see the family as a dynamic entity—constantly in flux—accepting and rejecting such diverse members of the community as the minister, the mother-in-law, the babysitter, the doctor, etc. (Polak, 1970). It is this natural group of people with whom we do our work.

The families we see are identified through an arrangement established with the coroners of Denver, Arapahoe, and Jefferson counties in Colorado. The families who consent to participate in the research project are being randomly assigned to a Crisis Intervention Experimental, or a No-Intervention Control Group. An additional matched group of families who have not experienced a recent death will serve as a No-Crisis Control Group.

Those families who have been assigned to the experimental group are contacted by the intervention team within at least 12 hours after the death. Usually, the team accompanies the medical examiner on his routine call to the home of the surviving family members. If the family agrees to participate in the study, they are seen for two to six sessions over a period of one to ten weeks, with the total family or social system being involved in the treatment. This short-term intervention is aimed at increasing the effectiveness of the family in coping with feelings, decisions, and subsequent adjustment related to the death.

Recognizing that there are many inherent problems in the evaluation of a broad-action

[1] Presented at the Annual Meeting, National Council on Family Relations, October 7-10, 1970, Chicago, Illinois.
[2] NIMH grant #MH 15867-02, Crisis Intervention: A Model for Primary Prevention. P. Polak (Project Director), R. M. Eisler and Leslie Jordan.

program, such as the present study, assessment is being geared more toward a field approach whereby the focus is not simply to test the hypotheses already formulated, but to suggest new ones as well. Thus, the assessment instruments were designed not only to obtain standard measures of outcome, but also to get qualitative and process-oriented data. The general areas chosen for evaluation are: (a) medical illness; (b) psychiatric illness; (c) family functioning; (d) crisis-coping behavior; and (e) social cost estimates. These areas will be measured six and eighteen months after the death for families in the Crisis Intervention Experimental and No-Intervention Control Groups. For the No-Crisis Control Group, the measures will be taken at initial contact with the families and again one year later.

It might seem presumptuous to describe assessment procedures and data collection when one stops to consider the problem created by strangers entering into a family system at a critical time, such as the event of a sudden and unexpected death. This problem gives a good illustration of the necessity of keeping in mind the fact that, just as an individual can be viewed as part of a family social system, the family must be seen as part of the larger social system. The manner in which a family incorporates societal values into its own familial value system has implications for family success or failure in readjustment after the death.

We have found our work to be most effective with those atomized, nuclear families, who are accustomed to the idea of professionals and experts from whom they willingly accept advice and support. These families have very direct lines to the mass society through its organs of communication and its accepted interactive patterns. They are club members, social churchgoers, and *Life magazine* readers, who conform enthusiastically to the expressed Weltanschauung of middle America. In the absence of the closely knit kin network of fifty years ago, they have their club and professional organization memberships; in the absence of neighborhood assistance, they hold considerable insurance against sudden need or tragedy; in the absence of grandmother's homilies on child-rearing, they have Haim Ginott; and in the absence of strong family traditions about death, they are open to expert intervention. The mortuary initially provides this professional guidance and sets norms. Its implicit messages include: "The 'body' is not to be touched"; "Be quiet—decorum is to be maintained"; or, "Experts are essential to the process surrounding death—to prepare the body, to properly bury it; you are unqualified in this area—defer to us." "To fulfill societal expectations," they say, "these things must be done." And they generally are, regardless of the emotional or monetary cost to the family. In the event of suicide, the family is most vulnerable. Suicide, unacceptable in the pervasive Judeo-Christian ethic, is seen as bringing shame to the family. As a result, natural mourning evoked by the loss is effectively blocked and superseded by guilt. Anger, which is normally veiled and only symbolically expressed in the larger culture to which they are finely attuned, likewise remains unexpressed. Further, anger toward a dead person is widely felt not to be legitimate and is only experienced with great discomfort.

These families, though in many cases financially well-prepared for death, are profoundly unprepared for its emotional impact. The topic of death creates a vague uneasiness which comes from a leery attitude toward aging, and an aseptic approach to the body. Death is the opposite of unblemished skin, white teeth, and regular bowel movements. The vast inexperience and overrefined sensibilities around the physical aspects of death preclude, in many cases, coming to grips with the emotional reality of eventual or immediate loss. These families, it seems, in the absence of secure and deeply ingrained patterns of coping with real-life crises, and in a situation where their cultural norms are minimal, inefficient, contradictory, or even nonexistent, have a battery of professionals on call to correct what otherwise would remain a raw and painful wound. The families have, in other words, a "contrived" social system from which semi-symbolic gratification of needs is provided on a new model, functionally suitable to current societal reality. Since they trust experts, knowing that they themselves are competent in only one or perhaps two fields, we are most cordially accepted into the "contrived" social system in which they move. As a result, we have been able to give much aid in terms of emotional support, advice, practical help, and guidance, but we have always had the feeling that they would have obtained other aid without much trouble had we been unavailable. These people are the successful "converters" of our culture.

There are, of course, families in the aforementioned group who interact a great deal with the larger social system, but do not become mirrors of it. They are able, on the one hand, to become aware of the cultural norms and values in the area of death, but somehow they are able to assimilate only those values consonant with the goals and priorities of the family system, discarding the others. On the other hand, this pattern of open but selective interaction makes many support systems, such as religious and fraternal organizations, friends and neighbors, etc., available to the bereaved family, permitting successful use of these resources.

With families who are part of a cohesive cultural subgroup, our success has been less than overwhelming. In contrast to the families mentioned above, we have been intimidated by the sheer number of mourners, by clearly competent friends and neighbors, and by the ease and grace with which these families function at the time of a death. We have found ourselves ornamental at best, and awkward, isolated bumblers at worst. We have been impressed with the fact that, in these families, children are not shunted aside, but carry on in their usual loosely supervised and irrepressible manner—crying, laughing, playing, or whatever. We have seen that the body is not isolated (nor referred to as the "body"), rather, it is touched and wept over freely. We have seen emotional needs met swiftly as they occur. It seems that families who are members of a cohesive subculture are clearly closed to the mass society, in terms of their supreme inability to adhere to the larger norms and values about death. Yet, in their small subculture, there exist norms which most adequately serve needs arising during a crisis of this sort, which allow for extreme expression of grief or anger, and, in general, accept feeling. In this natural structure comprised of family, friends, and neighbors, death becomes again what it once must have been—a highly functional rite of loss and grieving. In its immediate despair and disorganization, death is a deep confirmation of life and of the necessity of human cooperation.

There is still another group in which the families are atomized and nuclear, but interact neither with contrived nor natural social systems which might be called on for help in time of need. They have no club memberships, no huge kin system, no ministers, no bridge parties, and no neighbors who are known to them, even though there are people living on each side of them. In general, they have minimal social contact. They are tied up in their family exclusively, and any outside interests are regarded more as an intrusion than a pleasurable diversion. These isolates have every chance of incurring the physical and mental breakdown seen possible among survivors after a death. These families, with such meager resources, can bankrupt themselves in time of tragedy. It is our hypothesis that these are the families who need aid and support more than any others; but the task is difficult. Their resistance to outside help is as great as their need.

It would appear then, in general, that the degree to which families allow for and benefit from outside intervention is a function of their incorporation of the norms and values of the larger society into their own familial value system.

Up to this point, we have directed our attention to different ways in which two social systems—the family and society—interact, and the effect this has on how a particular family will respond to a death, as well as that family's willingness to accept and make use of outside intervention. Our focus will now shift to an examination of processes within the family that influence the course of bereavement and subsequent readjustment.

We have found that families with open internal communication systems are more prone to resist the societal taboos surrounding the area of death, and are thus more likely to discuss and make realistic plans for the death of their members. A family that consistently deals with stress by attempting to assess and absorb the reality components of the situation rather than by trying to deny them, is certainly able to cope more effectively with the immediate crisis that a sudden death precipitates. The degree to which it is permissable to express feelings of sadness and loss, as well as the less acceptable reactions of anger, guilt, and relief, seems to play a large role in determining the success of the readjustment period.

These coping patterns are examples of some variables of internal organization within the family system that affect the way it deals with the sudden and unexpected death of one of its members. Our experience to date shows, however, that the single most important factor in the reorganization of a family as a continuing social system following a death, is the role the decedent had been assigned, and which he assumed within the family system.

The resumption of adaptive functioning, following a death, is facilitated in a family where vital roles and functions have been apportioned among members in a just and equitable manner for optimal comfort and satisfaction in their performance. This type of apportionment occurs when roles are assumed according to individual need, ability, and potential. In such a case, role assumption is usually explicit and well-understood by all family members. When a member of this type of family dies, the critical period of reorganization is not likely to be experienced as a crisis because the family already has a built-in process which allows it to reallocate the role functions of the decedent with minimal difficulty.

No matter how equitable and explicit the role distribution in a family system, the exact number and type of roles held by the decedent influence the degree of difficulty experienced by that family in its attempts at readjustment. For example, in comparison to a child, an adult assumes primarily instrumental or task-oriented roles. Some of these, like the role of the breadwinner, can be troublesome and time-consuming to reallocate if the skills necessary to fill that role are not available among the surviving family members. On the other hand, the death of a child, while precipitating a lengthy and intense period of emotional stress, usually does not necessitate an extensive period of role reorganization, since children have roles that are primarily expressive or social-emotional in nature.

This is not to imply that expressive roles are easier to redistribute or that they can be left vacant for longer periods of time without repercussion. The death of a family member whose role was essentially expressive can often times lead to disaster, particularly if the function of that role was to camouflage or resolve a conflict existing within the family system. Take the death of a child, for example. If the child created a distance between the parents or, conversely, if he was a catalyst to stimulate otherwise dormant feelings in order to keep the family emotionally extant, his death would severely tax the family's already inadequate resources to deal with stress, provoking further disorganization and maladaptive behavior.

Expressive roles, particularly those that encompass some type of deviant or unacceptable behavior, are usually assumed on the basis of much more ambiguous criteria than age or sex. A role can be classified as deviant either by the particular norm system of the family or by the one that the larger society employs. If the family member that dies was always a little different from the others—if he never quite fit in—the phase of readjustment will be relatively brief and minimally stressful. This is because the decedent, prior to his death, had already been extruded from the family system, and had held a role perceived by the family as nonfunctional in terms of its own value system. Often it is the deviant, as defined by society, who plays a dysfunctional role in the family. Alcoholics, for example, sometimes become not only useless to their families in the sense of having ceased to provide either tangible or emotional support, but also become a liability in terms of draining family resources and provoking community censure. Their deaths demand little, if any, need for role reallocation in a family and often engender a sense of relief.

At other times, however, rather than being dysfunctional, the alcoholic, the suicide attempter, or the hysteric—any symptomatic person, in fact—performs one of the most vital role functions for the maintenance of the entire family structure. That crucial role is to symbolize and represent a disturbance in the family social system. The death of that person sets off a process in the family, parallel to symptom substitution in the individual. Symptom substitution has been described by some as the replacement of one set of behavior, thought to express or represent some inner conflict, by another set whose function is identical. This phenomenon occurs when the inner conflict is not resolved, but the symbolic representation of it in behavioral form is discouraged or extinguished in some manner. A similar process has been observed in the family social system. Many family therapists have documented the spontaneous development of symptoms in one family member when those of another member have shown remission during the course of treatment. When the symptomatic member of a family dies, however, his role is not redistributed so easily. His family system, already by definition functioning in a precarious and faulty fashion, will be forced to undergo an extensive and painful period of readjustment which, if unsuccessful, either in terms of reassigning his role or working through the original systems conflict, will eventuate in the collapse of the system.

This chapter has described a research project designed to test the effectiveness of crisis intervention techniques, as a model for primary prevention for bereaved families. We have discussed these families' immediate reactions to death and their subsequent reorganization in light of two factors: the interaction pattern that exists between the family and the larger social system, and the one that prevails within the family system itself. Our observations to date have suggested that the degree to which a family will accept and benefit from outside intervention at the time of a death is a function of its incorporation of the norms and values of society into its own familial value system. In addition, the type of system—coping patterns employed by the family, as well as the role the decedent had assumed within the family system, have been found to be critical variables that influence the course of bereavement and subsequent readjustment.

REFERENCES

Polak, P. Social systems intervention. *Archives of General Psychiatry*, 1970, (in press).
Rees, W. D., & Lutkins, S. G. Mortality of bereavement. *British Medical Journal*, 1967, 4, 13–16.

CHAPTER 10

SIDS:
The Survivor
as Victim

Eric Markusen
Greg Owen
Robert Fulton
Robert Bendiksen

In addressing the issues surrounding SIDS, an important question must be raised: Is there any reason to expect that the aftermath of a SIDS death may be more traumatic and problematic than that precipitated by death and loss of other kinds? Our comprehensive review of the literature enables us to answer this question with a decided "yes." We have found several features of the death-grief constellation created by SIDS which create a particularly difficult and hazardous aftermath both for the immediate family members and for various individuals involved in case management. In the following section, several of these features will be briefly examined.

Sudden Infant Death Syndrome (SIDS) Features

SUDDENNESS

The first feature of SIDS which may produce a particularly traumatic grief situation is its suddenness. Coming as it does entirely by surprise, the SIDS death gives the survivors absolutely no opportunity to prepare for the loss. This is in marked contrast to the situation found in other infant and child death situations, where a progressive disease process permits some emotional preparation in the form of anticipatory grief.

ABSENCE OF DEFINITE CAUSE

Secondly, the fact that no definite cause can be assigned to SIDS complicates the grief and recuperation of the survivors. The lack of a definite cause prevents a complete definition of the situation by the family and care-givers alike. In the absence of such a definition of the situation, the likelihood of intense guilt feelings increases, both because parents are given no definite rationale to feel blameless and because other persons, e.g., officials, friends, and relatives, can create doubts through criticisms of parental care, ignorance, etc.

PROBLEMATIC GRIEF REACTIONS: MOTHER-INFANT

A third reason that SIDS frequently precipitates problematic grief reactions is that it abruptly severs one of the most intense and important interpersonal relationships, namely, the mother-infant bond. After nine months of anticipation and preparation, the mother's (and father's) joy is crushed by the unexpected and unexplained death of their baby. That SIDS can create extremely harsh grief reactions has been documented by a recent study which found that women who have experienced a SIDS death have a much higher than average rate of infertility and spontaneous abortions in the months following the loss of their baby. One might add in conjunction with the above, that the loss of the baby is frequently the first experience with death for many young married couples. The lack of prior experience with death and grief combine with the unique difficulties posed by SIDS to render their grief and mourning particularly difficult.

SIBLING BEREAVEMENT

Fourth, SIDS not only imposes severe stress on the parents, but can create an especially difficult grief situation for bereaved siblings. When there are brothers or sisters involved, they must cope not only with their own bereavement, but also with their parents' grief. Numerous articles have emphasized the potential problems, such as irrational feelings of guilt and responsibility, faced by siblings, and have argued for more attention to these problems.

LEGAL SYSTEM INVOLVEMENT

A fifth aspect of SIDS which renders the grief of the survivors especially difficult lies in the fact that numerous individuals and agencies are likely to be involved in the case-management process. The problems encountered by grief-stricken parents forced to endure insensitive interrogations (and even incarcerations) by the police comprise a recurrent theme in the literature. The involvement of the legal system in cases of SIDS stems largely from the fact that the death is sudden and of unknown cause. Misconceptions about SIDS abound, and one of the most harmful is the association of SIDS with suffocation, both deliberate and accidental.

A recent nationwide survey of case management procedures by Dr. Abraham Bergman and his colleagues found that many communities have virtually no provision for attending to the needs of the survivors. Clearly, a great deal of support is required in order to provide satisfactory services to the survivors of SIDS.

It is hoped that the foregoing discussion will document our conviction that the survivors of SIDS are indeed victims in need of sensitive care and support. So devastating are the problems faced by the survivors of SIDS that a solid case can be made for establishing research into the issues surrounding survivorship of SIDS as having a priority commensurate with that presently accorded to studies of causation.

The personal and social costs of SIDS do not end with the tragic loss of thousands of infant lives; nor with the agonized grief imposed upon many more thousands of survivors. In addition to these tolls, SIDS presents a critical challenge to the skills and resources of the helping professions. Several features of SIDS create problems for the concerned care-giver.

PROBLEMS FOR CONCERNED CARE-GIVER

First, individuals on the scene of a SIDS death (usually rescue squads, police officers, or hospital emergency room staff) must cope with an intense emotionally-charged situation involving an unexpected death from an unknown cause. Invalid stereotypes or misconceptions on the part of personnel involved at this point can lead to imputations of parental culpability if not outright accusations of infanticide. The risk of intensifying the shock and guilt of survivors is great. A combination of informed compassion, tact, and ability to perform the necessary service is required. Special educational programs would undoubtedly reduce harmful misconceptions concerning SIDS and thereby increase the helping potential of legal or other agents at the scene.

Second, there is a fine line between concerned and helpful intervention at a time of acute crisis and an imposition or intrusion on the privacy of the family. Initial contacts with recently bereaved families must be undertaken with great care, in order for vital information to be gathered and provision of services to be offered. In this context, the availability of organized groups of SIDS survivors in both consulting and service capacities is greatly valued.

Third, the nature of SIDS requires the interface among individuals representing various agencies and professions. Given the variety of perspectives and responsibilities in a comprehensive SIDS service system, the need for open communication and exchange of information and assistance becomes imperative. SIDS poses a crucial challenge to the various legal, medical, and helping professions to devise an interdisciplinary service system of maximum value to the survivors of SIDS. An immediate need in the development of services for SIDS survivors is the identification of potential participants in a care-giving role. In this respect, the funeral director is in an excellent position to provide information to SIDS survivors as well as note situations in which pathological grief reactions are suspected.

Recent studies have shown the potential worth of the funeral director in the care of survivors. By virtue of the fact that the funeral director is an early member of the care-giving team, and one who is on the scene at the request of the family, he has an opportunity to play an important supportive role. First, he is in immediate and direct contact with the grieving survivors at the time of their loss. Second, his presence generally is not seen as an intrusion in the affairs of the family. Third, by virtue of his role as funeral director, he can help to channel the survivors' grief along positive and reconstructive lines.

Equally important, in his interface with the clergy, physicians, nurses, and other health care personnel, he can be an important figure in the care and support of the bereaved family in the critical weeks and months following their loss.

It would be germane to any intervention program which might be proposed to:

1. assess the sensitivity of the funeral director to the role that he might play with respect to SIDS;
2. determine the manner in which that role might be successfully managed; and
3. study actual case histories to evaluate the effectiveness of varying modes of intervention.

Enough is known about grief to stimulate the establishment of preliminary intervention programs. What is lacking is the collection of systematic and definitive data on normal and abnormal grief processes. It is only recently, moreover, that there has been a scientific effort to understand the long-term impact of loss. An objective evaluation of proposed intervention programs would add to our knowledge and understanding of grief processes and the potential maladaptive responses of bereaved survivors.

CHAPTER 11

Repressed Affect
and
Memory Reactive
to Grief:
A Case Fragment

David K. Switzer

The operation of the mechanisms of denial and the repression of affect and even of memory surrounding the death of a person with whom one has been closely tied emotionally has been noted and described before. The purpose of this report of the losses of a 20-year-old psychiatric patient is not to go through the superfluous activity of seeking to demonstrate that such repression *can* happen, but to portray a rather unique combination of such repressions that had the effect of producing an almost total amnesia for the details of a relationship which had existed since the patient's birth. A second purpose is to introduce in the context of this case a methodology for the facilitation of grief work which can be utilized not only in severe cases such as this, but which is adaptable to the counseling procedures in dealing with "normal" grief, beginning at the time of the loss, and therefore hopefully preventive of "morbid" grief reactions.

This 20-year-old woman was admitted to a psychiatric hospital on the basis of about five months of moderate depression reactive to a series of events: anticipatory grief during the several-month terminal illness of her grandfather, with whom she had had an unusually close emotional relationship, the breaking off of a romance by her boyfriend, and the death of her grandfather about a month later.

The patient was the first child of her parents. A congenital disorder required rather constant attention, continuing because of parental anxiety even after the disorder was corrected. This attention was drastically and suddenly curtailed when the patient was about three by the birth of the next sibling, and then a third. One can presume the sense of deprivation.

When the patient was 15, she left her own home to live with her maternal grandparents in the same city, the reason given being the availability in another high school of a better department in the field of her major interest. In this home she was the exclusive center of attention, reproducing the situation of the first three years of her life.

The contemporary events of loss began with the grandfather's hospitalization with cancer. Although the patient knew of this, she was not informed of its critical nature until she was actually in the car going to visit him for the first time several weeks after his admission. This tardy statement did not prepare her at all for the shock of seeing his debilitated body and his inability even to recognize her. She remained in the room only briefly, recoiling in horror. She never returned to see him.

Within several weeks the young man with whom she was in love simply stopped seeing her and calling her. When the impact of this broken relationship hit her, she made a mild suicide attempt, rather obviously communicative-manipulative in nature, reflective of her genuine feelings of abandonment and despair, but reporting later that there was the equally genuine feeling of not wanting to kill herself *dead*.

Within another few weeks the grandfather died. The precise beginning point of her depression could not be identified. It had been in the process of development and never lifted, although she was never totally nonfunctional in it. After about three more months, during which she saw a psychiatrist several times, she was admitted to the hospital.

It was judged that although there was an underlying, long-term, and deep emotional need that would call for continued treatment, a noticeable raising of mood and mobilization of ego resources might be accomplished by means of intensive crisis therapy focusing on her recent experiences of loss, since, with the exception of the acting out of the suicide attempt, they had never been openly expressed. It was hypothesized that the loss of the grandfather was primary, first, chronologically, because it in fact dated from her experience in the hospital room, and second, because it was a life-long relationship. It was not implausible to think that her anticipatory grief reactions were of such a nature as to have played some role in the withdrawal of the boyfriend, although there are no data to substantiate such a presupposition.

The procedure was to see her twice a week, 45 minutes to an hour, for three weeks, with an exclusive focus being on her grief reaction to the loss of her grandfather; then, if progress were made, to move to the loss of the boyfriend and the suicide gesture. The therapeutic relationship and the methodology employed were based upon the needs of bereaved persons and the rationale for stimulating the griefstricken to talk as soon as possible and as fully as possible about the dead person, the relationship, and the death events. This material is elaborated in another place (Switzer, 1970). With this patient a clear contract was made concerning the focus and the number of sessions. Such a contract would not ordinarily be made in the usual, or the nonpathological, grief reaction, when one presumes that the grief work will be done with several persons, in several structured and nonstructured social settings, and over a period of several months.

A very strong distrust of and anger at the hospital on the part of the patient was evident at the beginning and continued throughout the interviews. However, the therapist was not officially related to the hospital, and the young woman was genuinely responsive to the attempt of someone to talk with her about her grandfather, something that she had avoided, but felt was important.

The first task was to seek to elicit the affect which one would normally expect during the time of anticipatory grief and the initial grief reaction itself through the exploration of the illness, the death, and the immediate postdeath experiences, including the funeral. This beginning point is based upon the rather well-established evidence that the shock and denial which is the usual first reaction to the death of an emotionally related person is the attempt to deal with the intense anxiety of loss and its threat to the self. In most instances, shock and denial are not capable of handling the combined power of the internal feelings and the external reality of the death. The next normal phase of grief, then, is an outpouring of emotion, the feeling and expression of pain, the variety of emotions not always clearly differentiated and identified at this point, but yet a rather uninhibited cathartic expression. When this has not taken place, as it had not with this patient, further stages of grief work cannot be accomplished. Therefore the methodology of the therapist is to ask the grief sufferer to recount as much detail as possible about the death and the events surrounding it, pressing always for more detail and for the expression of the feelings which the person might have been experiencing at the time. This is a very directive, sensitively aggressive lancing of a psychic wound that is still festering. To use terms like directive and aggressive is not at all in conflict with the central role of the accurate communication of empathy which is seen by Carkhuff (1969) and others as the absolutely essential ingredient of all effective helping relationships.

Following this cathartic expression, and including inevitably the beginning of self-exploration concerning the relationship between the grieved person and the deceased, one's feelings about one's self and the other, a complete review of the relationship is the next appropriate phase. There are the needs, first, as so many writers have pointed out, to release one's self from the external ties to the lost person; second, to reaffirm one's self as a worthwhile person; and third, to rekindle as presently potent earlier good images, those internalized aspects of the other and of the relationship which had been at an earlier time need gratifying (Switzer, 1970). Again, the procedure is to take an active role in asking the bereaved person about the deceased, about him as a person, about their relationship, asking again in detail for all of the possible significant memories, what they did together, what they said, what the bereaved person felt at the time, the meaning of all of this for him.

With the young woman suffering from depression, an unexpected barrier was discovered almost from the very beginning. Not only was she presently unable to respond with the appropriate affect, not only had she repressed the actual feelings, but she had repressed even the memory of having had feelings at all, the memory of most of the events surrounding her grandfather's death, and *almost all memory of the events of her lifelong relationship with him.* The selective nature of this memory loss must be emphasized, because memory loss in general was not a part of her clinical picture. It was only in regard to her grandfather.

She did recall the shock of seeing in the hospital what she reported as the wasted away body of what had been her grandfather ("It was not really him." Denial.), his inability even to recognize her, and her leaving the room to vent her anger at her family for not having prepared her for this and for their present open discussion of his impending death (her response to what was seen by her as a challenge to her denial). She could remember her father's telling her of the grandfather's death, but could neither presently feel nor recall her feelings at the time. She went to the funeral home alone, refusing to go with any of the family, reporting that she would not put herself in the position of being with anyone else when she was feeling deeply and might have to express her emotions in their presence. ("It's a sign of weakness.") When questioned persistently about what she experienced when she stood alone before his body, it was interesting to note that she responded fairly readily; her only memory of affect was that of anger, ("I was mad at him because he had left my grandmother alone.") It was only in a later session that she was able to say that she was angry at him for leaving *her.*

As far as the funeral was concerned, the patient remembered attending, but details of the event and her feelings before, during, and after were not available to her.

This type of directive probing was carried out through persistent and specific questioning, reflective responses attentive to affect, and statements which were intended to be invitational to affect. ("I think if I were in such a situation I would feel . . ." "That would make me feel . . .") This type of statement would tend to have the effect of giving permission to feel and express loss, guilt, sadness, anger. Three aspects of the patient's behavior during this first session need to be noted. First, she was not without feeling, apathetic. Several times feelings would begin to rise to the surface in the direction of expression and would be cut off. To the extent that these were attempts to *remember* and *relive* feelings at the time of the grandfather's illness and death, the mechanism seemed to be that of repression. When the affect was genuinely contemporary, right now as she talked, it was much more conscious suppression, prior conditioning to fight one's own feelings and not to let them out for others or even one's own self to see and experience fully. Second, she herself seemed genuinely astonished and baffled by her inability to remember what had gone on and how she had felt, as if she had put out of her mind up until this point that she even *should* try to remember. Third, positive transference toward the therapist began to develop quite rapidly.

In the second session, the therapist made the decision to move on to the second phase of grief counseling, that of reviewing the whole relationship between the grief sufferer and the dead person, even though obviously phase one was incomplete. It was judged that further direct confrontation with the events of the death would meet with continued unconscious resistance, and, since time was limited, that the approach to the painful emotions might be made by withdrawing to earlier, more pleasant memories. Then the therapist could lead the patient chronologically back to the illness and death, with the ego now being strengthened by some reinforcement of earlier "good objects." Also during this second phase, the relationship between the patient and the therapist could continue to develop and perhaps aid in facilitating the exploration of the repressed painful affect. The grandfather had been discussed in quite idealistic terms. The relationship with him had been a most meaningful one during all of her life. When she was a child they had done many things together. In her teens she lived with him and they talked about many things. He was always there. He was available, but *he did not bother her or make demands of her.* Following the principle of concreteness as a necessary facilitative condition for effective psychotherapy (Carkhuff, 1969), the patient was asked to describe specifically and in detail events in her relationship with her grandfather. What did they do together? What did they talk about? Recount times together, activities, conversation. The first response, with some amazement to herself, was, "I don't know. I can't. I can't remember." After persistent pushing by the therapist for memories and images, only four could be reproduced. One, when the patient was small, he took her to the carnival a few times. Two, he took her fishing a few times, but in fact, she did not like to go fishing. Three, she could remember him in his chair watching television. Four, she talked with him about her problems, but pressing for detail revealed that it was actually her *grandmother* who talked with her. No more information was forthcoming concerning what had taken place between them, except that she was quite clear that at no time, even when she was small, did they express their affection for one another in any physical way. Time and again throughout the interview, the patient's reply was, "I don't remember. I just can't.'"

This degree of memory repression is considerably more than ordinary, extending beyond just the affect and painful events of the death itself to the patient's entire lifetime of relationship with her grandfather, but which, except for a few small fragments, she was unable to document in concrete terms. One might begin to speculate that in addition to the rather obvious repression operating, much of the relationship between the two was one of fantasy and idealization on the part of the patient, not new fantasy and idealization as a part of the grief reaction, which, of course, does happen, but extending from her childhood days, as she sought available love (i.e., need fulfilling) objects in response to perceived rejection by her parents. A picture of the grandfather began to emerge, as much as the therapist could piece together the reality of it, of a man who was rather passive and undemonstrative, who placed no demands on his granddaughter, who could then be viewed in contrast with the parents and idealized. In addition, her own emotional life seemed to be patterned very much after his, the suppression of affection, not allowing the "weakness" of feeling and its expression: identification with part aspects of the real man as well as the idealized man.

The patient's rather rapid positive transference seemed to be in terms of her feelings toward her grandfather, assisted by the actual role of the therapist as administratively unrelated to the hospital, the negative transference already having been directed at the hospital as personified by her administrative psychiatrist. This double transference was rather strongly demonstrated when she sought to maneuver the therapist into the position of taking her side against the hospital, saving her by aiding in her discharge, an apparent reenactment of the utilization of grandparent against parent. The maneuvering ended when the therapist proposed this interpretation of the behavior he was observing and pointed out that the reality of the present situation was such that he could not fulfill this role and that this would not fit their original contract. The full import of the interpretation did not gain immediate full acceptance, but both the comparison of the relationships and the present reality were understood, and it was possible to move on with the grief work.

This point in the fourth session marked the beginning of a breakthrough in the expression of feeling when based on the recognition of the meaning of the present relationship. The therapist reminded the patient that they would have only two more sessions, then he, too, would leave her, a repetition of loss. This focus on what was happening at the present moment is the introduction of immediacy as defined by Carkhuff (1969). It produced a series of affective responses, beginning with tears and the statement, "Everyone I really care about leaves me." She was able to say that she was hurting over the anticipation of the separation from the therapist. In this context, she began to discuss how difficult it was for her to say "goodbye," followed by the first realization that she had not told her grandfather goodbye, knowing now that she could have visited him earlier in the hospital, that she did not because of her own need to deny what was taking place, accepting her responsibility and beginning to feel her guilt about it. Once again she reflected upon seeing his body at the funeral home and feeling anger "because he had left me alone," the "me" replacing the "grandmother" of her earlier statement. It was suggested that she might well have feelings of anger at the therapist at the present time because he was leaving her, but she reported not experiencing this.

The fifth session picked up on the separation theme and how people separate from one another. An attempt was made by the therapist to enable her to say goodbye to her grandfather now, both by asking the question, "What would you like to tell him now?" ("I don't know."), and then asking her to see the therapist as the grandfather and talk directly to him ("I can't do it."). Finally, the therapist asked, "How are you going to say goodbye to me?" Again, "I don't know," but the deep expression of hurt, and her tears began to show that she was opening up to the possibility of *feeling* her emotions and expressing them openly and directly. The next procedural steps in the last session would be to attempt to link this present relationship, the separation, and the experiencing and expression of this loss and its goodbye, including its hurt, threat, and anger, to what went on at the loss of her grandfather and her boyfriend.

Before the final session her parents came to the hospital, requested her discharge, and took her home. She and the therapist never said goodbye.

REFERENCES

Carkhuff, Robert R. *Helping and human relations.* New York: Holt, Rinehart and Winston, (Volumes I and II), 1969.

Switzer, David K. *The dynamics of grief.* Nashville: Abingdon, 1970.

PART 3
The Relationships
of
Health Professionals

Many kinds of professionals work with the dying and the bereaved: funeral directors, chaplains and clergy, social workers and psychologists, dieticians, health educators, lawyers, and others, but the most familiar are usually the health caretakers: physicians, nurses, health care administrators, home health service staff, and other health professionals. For this reason, more attention has been given to health caretakers than to other professionals.

As a result of the immense importance of health professionals, these individuals receive the greatest numbers of compliments and the greatest numbers of complaints. Physicians in particular, whose training is primarily in clinical medicine, are often faulted for not also being capable in the human relations aspects of their work with dying patients. There is evidence that the awareness and sensitivity of physicians to these persons is increasing; at the same time, others in the health fields are taking over some of the human relations tasks.

The hospice movement, begun in England and spread rapidly around the world, has provided one extremely significant alternative to the usual hospital care of dying persons, especially in terms of reduced costs and improved human care. A hospice is a facility that provides both inpatient and outpatient care to persons whose physicians have determined that cure is no longer possible. Hospice staff and volunteers focus their efforts on keeping the dying person in his or her home environment as long as possible; when home care is no longer feasible, an inpatient hospice-related facility continues to offer services that emphasize pain control, autonomy, and access to friends and family members.

Often ignored in the care of the dying is the stress felt by their caretakers. Whether physicians or nursing aids, it is too easy to forget that working with dying persons is extremely stressful for health caretakers, even those who have relatively little on-going contact with the patients. Increasing concern has been expressed that these individuals too must have the opportunity for some kind of support, either through their own support networks or through a formal service provided by the hospital, hospice, or other community facility.

The role of the health professional has to be recognized as part of the entire health system, which includes social institutions, physical plants, funding sources, political institutions, value systems, and all the individual and idiosyncratic aspects of the persons who work or otherwise function in the system. Our nation has made remarkable strides in the clinical medical care of all persons, and it is now making strides in the psychosocial care of dying persons.

CHAPTER 12

Nursing Care of
the Terminal Patient

Sandra Simmons and Barbara Given

Since the early 1960's, there have been numerous articles in nursing literature dealing with the topic of death, yet there is still a noticeable lack of empirical study of a group of dying patients to determine their nursing needs. Many articles and studies are accounts of one nurse caring for one dying patient and relating her experience with that patient (Carson, 1971; Eisman, 1971; Hoffman, 1971). Other articles deal with attitudes of patients and personnel about the topic of death (Quint, 1967; Sudnow, 1965). Nurses must get more involved in researching and reporting clinical findings if they are to prove that nursing can and does offer a unique service to the dying patient.

The most crucial phase in dying begins when there is "nothing more to do" for the patient. This means that the patient has no chance of recovery. At this point the medical goal changes from recovery to comfort (Glaser & Strauss, 1965). It then becomes the nurse's role to assume major responsibility for care by ensuring patient comfort. Yet, the work of the sociologists and psychologists suggest that nurses respond to patients at this point with lessened involvement (Glaser & Strauss, 1965, p. 227). The nurse's prime concern may become meeting her comfort needs; thus, she may administer pain medications too freely to keep the dying patient "comfortable" and quiet. If relating with the patient, the nurse may tend to use an overly cheerful or superficial approach in an attempt to maintain complete control of the interaction and not get involved; however, direct patient care is usually ascribed to the non-professional or semi-professional personnel. When direct patient contact must be made by the registered nurse, she may tend to focus on objects, tasks, or equipment rather than the patient as a person. By decreasing her involvement with the patient, the nurse facilitates the maintenance of her own composure in a situation where the goal of recovery has been altered. This prevents or decreases involvement and feelings of loss, sadness, or inadequacy when death does occur. A typical nursing response as to why the patient's death or dying is not discussed is, "He doesn't want to talk about it."

To determine if the terminal patient would talk about his death and dying, a small study was conducted focusing on the verbalization of the terminally ill patient. It was hypothesized that the dying patient would express feelings about his own death if given the opportunity. An analysis of these expressions should then provide insight into some of the needs and feelings of the terminal patient and give direction for determining the kind of care nurses should provide to meet these needs. This information could be used in educating present and future nurses in some aspects of working with dying patients.

The patients selected for this study were from medical and surgical units in one general hospital. The interviews were carried out over a three-month period. The criteria for patient selection were: (1) a terminal illness that would probably be fatal within six months; (2) minimum age of sixteen years—no maximum age limit; (3) rational and oriented. The interviewer was not a regular member of the nursing staff and was unknown to most of the patients. Some of the patients had seen the interviewer in her role as a nursing faculty member. Length of interviews varied from 15 to 45 minutes depending upon the patient's condition or interruptions. An interview guide was used to insure uniformity in the data collection. After the interview, additional information was collected from the chart, nursing staff, and Kardex.

The study included thirty-two males and nineteen females ranging in age from twenty to eighty-eight years. All patients interviewed were terminal cancer patients. The major body systems affected by cancer were: genitourinary, gastrointestinal, pulmonary, and hematologic. Expressions about death and dying came from forty-seven of the fifty-one patients interviewed. Some expressions were direct using the terms death and dying, such as "I want to stop thinking of dying," while other references were implied such as "when this is all over," "I'm tired of lingering," "this is my last time in the hospital," or "will I ever go home?"

Examination of the patients' charts showed only five instances of nurses' recording any expression, direct or implied, of death or dying. No notations of this fact were found on the Kardex; however, on eight Kardex cards it was noted that no emergency resuscitation should be initiated. There were no notations on chart or Kardex indicating whether or not the patient knew or discussed his diagnosis with the staff. On one chart a social worker had noted that the patient knew his diagnosis.

The data collected seems to indicate that the terminally ill patient will discuss his death and illness if given the opportunity. Even though there were four patients who did not discuss their death with the interviewer, they did talk about their illness to some extent. These four patients were quite close to death, and it appeared that they had detached themselves from their surroundings. In these instances, death occurred within two to eight days following the attempted interview. It is interesting to note that the patient's emotional feelings about his illness and/or death were expressed within the first 10 to 15 minutes of the interview. Also of interest is the fact that the patient had such a need to express his feeling that he did so to a stranger without concern or fear of exposure.

In two separate instances, this interviewer observed patients being told that there was nothing more medically that could be done and that death was near. In both instances, the patient engaged anyone near in conversation about his terminal state, including physicians unknown to the patient who happened to be in the hall, visitors, other patients, cleaning ladies, and most of all, the nursing personnel. It is true that certain precipitating factors (transfusions; death of friend, family member, or roommate) may cause the patient to have an immediate and unforeseen need to express his feelings about death, dying, or his illness; however, it would seem that more often than not this need could be predicted and met by the nursing staff. In some instances it does seem that this need is identified by the staff so they can avoid the patient at this time. The question that arises is—if the patient's need to express himself were being met by the nursing staff, would 47 out of 51 patients interviewed have talked about their death or dying to an interviewer unknown to them?

Of the fifty-one patients interviewed only seven had the same nursing personnel assigned to their care two days in succession. More significant was the fact that in most instances the direct care of these patients was given by non-professional nursing personnel who have little if any formal preparation or experience in dealing with emotional problems or assessing psychological needs. An astute nurse who is familiar with the patient should be able to detect overt and covert behavioral manifestations of anxiety. Some patients do not discuss their illness openly but allude to it. Others may describe their illness in great detail initially so as to orient a new person to their personal feelings and problems and thereafter never refer to the illness again. This patient wants others to know that he is aware and well informed but does not choose to discuss the subject. Some patients show anxiety by frequently questioning personnel about pain, therapy, drugs, or their disease. To identify a pattern, one must be familiar with the patient and his behavior over a few days' period of time, as well as know what factual information the patient has been told by the physician or others on the health team.

Assessment of needs is as important for the terminal patient as it is for any other patient. If one is to provide comfort and treat the patient as an individual, he must know the patient's concerns and attitudes toward his illness and death. The nurse must determine the patient's stage of awareness so that the response is appropriate (Glaser & Strauss, 1965; Kubler-Ross, 1969). This is best done when a member of the nursing staff spends sufficient time with the patient to develop meaningful rapport and relationships with him.

Of the seven patients who had the same member of the nursing staff assigned to care for them frequently, three pointed out how valuable and good it was to have someone who knew how to make them more comfortable, someone who knew how to move them and get them up without causing unnecessary pain. One patient related how the practical nurse knew when to bathe her and when she needed to rest longer. She stated that others came in and did her care when they wanted to rather than when she wanted it done. Another patient stated "there are only three people here who know what is right for me." The patient knows if he can talk to the nurse, if she is in a hurry, or if she is willing to listen to him. Only after establishing these facts is the patient willing to trust and feel safe in initiating a conversation on an emotionally charged subject such as his illness or dying.

Another patient had been cared for over a long period of time by a practical nurse who freely discussed death and dying with him. About two hours before he died the patient asked the practical nurse to call his family and then to come and sit with him. She stayed with him and they discussed his dying and he related that he was afraid and didn't want to be left alone. After sitting with him for about twenty minutes, he asked the practical nurse what it would be like to be dead. She stated that she really did not know because she had never experienced it but that her father had always told her that life was just one step from death and death was just one step "through the door." He seemed satisfied with this answer. His family came and the practical nurse left. Ten minutes before he died he asked his family to leave, stating that he was ready to be alone. He died peacefully, calmly, alone, and apparently content. This continuous nurse-patient relationship had provided the necessary components to identify and meet his patient's needs.

Assignment of the appropriate member of the nursing team to a patient over a period of time is one important aspect in providing continuity of care. Though it is true that the length of time spent with the patient is not as important as the quality of the relationship, it does provide an opportunity for insight that can be obtained in no other way. Another factor to consider is that it is easier for the person giving the care to adjust to a different assignment daily than for the patient to adjust to a new staff member daily (indeed three times a day as he may have at least one new person each shift). The high degree of flux and uncertainty the dying patient is experiencing does not need to be compounded by asking him to adjust to different personnel daily on each shift.

In addition to providing continuity through stabilization of assignments, there should be some assurance that the time spent with the patient is focused on more than just carrying out a task. Physical care is planned for patients prior to its administration. In the same manner why shouldn't there be planned conversation? Planned conversation does not mean that the entire conversation should be planned in detail but thought should be given to information to be discussed during the time spent with the patient. Planned listening refers to wholehearted listening to determine what needs or cues the patient expresses that may be relevant to nursing care. By listening carefully to the phraseology, observing behavior, observing relationships with others, and interpreting silent messages, one can learn much about the patient's readiness to exchange and relate information.

Planned listening may support the patient in another way. Personnel can serve as a sounding board for the patient having to make critical decisions. At times the physician gives the patient information and the patient wants to talk about the implications. Examples of this from this study include a patient who was told that her treatment, if successful, would case side effects such as losing her hair, and possibly more blood disorders. Her concern in making the decision to start the treatment was whether her hair would come back, how easy it was to obtain a wig, and how to care for the wig. Listening and providing answers about wig care seemed to help her make her decision.

Another patient was scheduled for hypophysectomy for pain relief. She had no questions, just multiple expressions as to whether or not to have the surgery. Her fear was that of being a "vegetable." Mr. B. with bone cancer had a choice between two types of nerve resections for the relief of pain. In one type there was a question of incomplete relief while with the more extensive procedure there was a chance of paresis along with more assurance of pain relief. His conversation, without asking for answers, included all the pros and cons he could think of for each type of surgery. When the interview was over, he thanked the interviewer for being supportive while he was trying to make his decision and apologized for sounding confused. Another patient was interviewed just after the physician had told her that she had leukemia and that chemotherapy would probably not be effective. When encouraged to talk, she related various thoughts at random. After a while she said, "I feel okay now; you don't have to stay any longer." The next day she indicated that she felt much better and related how she hoped to spend some of her remaining time. Note that none of these patients wanted the interviewer to make the decision for him or give answers; each wanted to express himself aloud to facilitate his own decision-making. The staff should know what problems face patients and plan time in their care schedules to listen or help direct the patient's thoughts just as much as time is planned to give medications, do treatments, or chart.

Purposeful interacting cannot be carried out effectively behind barriers (Glaser & Strauss, 1965, pp. 226-256). Determining if and when the patient wants to talk is a challenge. Conversational cues must be picked up and pursued. Patients talk about topics they feel free to discuss and change subjects or avoid topics they do not want to discuss. By deliberate listening, the channels of communication can be kept open for the patient who desires to talk. It is difficult when we do not know what the patient really knows, what the physician has told him, or what others have said; but it behooves us to discuss this with the physician, the family, and to record on the chart or nursing care plan what the patient knows, the type of questions he asks, or his perception of his illness. Direct answers may be given if indicated but reflective questioning is preferred as a means of encouraging the patient to ventilate.

The terminal patient will indicate by his questions the kind of answers and amount of information he wishes. If he needs to deny, he should be allowed to maintain this emotional defense (Kubler-Ross, 1969, p. 34). He should not be forced to face unpleasant and unbearable situations that he cannot tolerate. If he asks, "Am I going to die?" he may be seeking support for his denial. He should never be told a lie but could be answered in some way that does not force reality on him at a time when he cannot tolerate it. At a later time he may ask "how much longer do I have to live?" suggesting that he can now tolerate a somewhat more specific answer.

When possible, the patient's question should be reflected or restated, thus allowing the opportunity for further expression. The nurse should be less concerned about what to say and more interested in how to listen. Then one can determine better what can be said to help the patient. Simple explanations usually suffice. First, find out what the patient really wants to know before answering. But above all, when answering be honest and straightforward. The terminal patient needs to be able to "trust" his physician, family, and staff. This appears to be necessary to assure him that everyone is really trying to help. Patients indicated lack of trust by stating that they were given "stock" answers, less time was spent with them, or lies were told to them. Mr. A. said "before, they told me it wasn't cancer and it was—so I won't believe anything now." Another patient said that she asked if she would ever go home again and they said "oh yes." However, the patient stated, "I'm getting worse, so I really don't see how I can." One patient related that when she was in a large medical center she was afraid and the nurse said "Don't worry. See that young school teacher? She taught school all year, is married and has a child and is doing very well. Now don't you be upset." The patient continued, "Yet during the six weeks that I was there, the other patient was readmitted to the hospital twice. I heard her beg her husband to kill her, to marry someone else so that she could know her daughter would have a mother. I heard her ask him why she had to suffer so." The patient said "I want people to be blunt and straightforward with me. Why can't they be?"

In some instances the patients seemed relieved to be able to express their feelings to someone who would listen objectively without trying to convince them that things would be all right. Mr. C. asked his family to leave and told a student nurse that he had to do this because they acted "funny" around him. He stated that they all came and kept talking about future plans and trips they would all take next summer. He stated that they had never done this before and that he couldn't understand the way they talked and acted. Mr. R. expressed how his family sat around and talked and "made me and themselves nervous; I had to tell them to go home." Another patient related how his family and the staff kept telling him not to give up and that things would work out. One patient related she could not talk to the two persons closest to her: her husband and her daughter. "I don't want to upset my daughter because she always cries and my husband keeps saying that I'll get well this time like I have before. He's hoping so hard I don't want to depress him."

If a dying patient has indirectly indicated to the nursing personnel he is ready to talk and finds no one picks up his cues, he may resort to a direct or startling question to gain attention. Two patients interviewed used such an approach. One asked, "What do you know about chemotherapy?"; the other "What is terminal cancer?" The first patient related her own knowledge about chemotherapy when the question was reflected; however, the second patient did not respond to the reflective approach and the interviewer answered the question. The direct answer was brief, yet straightforward and honest. It was a trying and difficult situation for the interviewer, and it is easy to see why some nurses withdraw from the conversation, put the patient off, or are not truthful in their response. Another poor response in this type of situation arises when the nurse answers the patient's question in great detail giving the patient far more information than he wanted or with which he is able to cope.

Often patients do not expect or want elaborate conversations from the staff; they just want to vent their feelings (Goldfarb, 1963, p. 635). Over one-third of the patients used the time with the interviewer to review their lives—to point out their contributions and accomplishments. They told what they had done, how full their lives had been, what sacrifices they had made for their children, and what a close relationship they had with their spouse. These expressions may be a way of convincing themselves that they fulfilled their duties and responsibilities and were ready to die or that they really hadn't been cheated out of life. The younger patient may spend his final days making arrangements for those who survive him so that in some way he will live in them and his relationship will continue after him (Goldfarb, 1963, p. 621; White, 1969, p. 638). If he lives on in memory, he feels that he is not completely removed and this makes dying more tolerable. It appears necessary not to deny the patient this aspect of the dying—or terminal—process.

Other patients review their lives from a more negative standpoint pointing out that they have many things left to do. Several related their responsibilities to their children, the need to care for their husbands, and two wanted to see the accomplishments of their children. Several stated that they were being cheated out of living even though in three cases the patient was over sixty years old. Another patient stated she regreted having traveled so much and having no roots. This left her "without a place to call home—to die in."

Often seemingly innocent remarks made by the staff may be misinterpreted by the patient. Mrs. B. was visited daily for three weeks by her minister who had served as a source of great support during her depression following surgery. Seeing the minister in the room one day the doctor said to him, "May I see you after you've finished your visit?" Mrs. B. interpreted this to mean that there was some adverse news about her progress, and she became apprehensive and frightened. All the doctor wanted to do was thank the minister for the part he played in helping her; yet during the interval between the original statement made by the doctor and its explanation to Mrs. B., she had experienced much unnecessary anxiety.

In the same way patients sometimes magnify the significance of what the nurse says or fails to say. Mrs. J. had inoperable cancer of the lung, and during one visit she related, "I know I'm getting worse. When I first came in the doctors and nurses told me I was 'looking better today,' but they don't ever say anything now so I must be worse." These examples demonstrated that the terminal patient searches for hidden meanings or constructs his own interpretation to events or information he does not understand. Thus, it is paramount for nurses to predict and prevent or rapidly correct this.

Literature indicated that the thought of dying is made tolerable by the patient's maintenance of hope—the door of possible recovery must be kept open (Feifel, 1959, p. 253; Kubler-Ross, 1969, p. 122). Patients in this study were constantly looking for clues or hope which seem to offer them comfort and provide a nourishment for living. Some patients perceive a decrease in pain or edema, an increase in appetite, a decrease in jaundice, or a new drug being tried as positive signs of their progress. Each day as reality closes in the hope becomes smaller. Each losing of possibilities may bring pain or loss and a redefinition of life and purpose. One should not hold out hope that is gone nor should one minimize what is left. Some expressions of hope voiced by those interviewed included:

"Dr. S. gives me hope—I don't know what I'd do without that."

"One tumor is getting smaller from the cobalt so maybe there is some hope."

"Chemotherapy will give me the best odds."

"I can eat much better here and with that new drug Dr. S. ordered. I have no nausea and vomiting and have even gained two pounds."

"It won't be so bad having this malignancy if the surgery decreases the pain."

"Dr. W. is now giving me this drug, yet last week he said he didn't think there was anything he could do for me. There must be a chance."

The nurse's role is to see that the patient does maintain realistic hope. The need for continued life is basic for goal oriented behavior. Bleak prospects result in feelings of emptiness, isolation, apathy, and potential self destruction. It is vital to have a will to live to face the remainder of life constructively. One patient said, "As long as I have hope the drug will work, I can continue; when that is gone, I couldn't tolerate living." Often the maintenance of hope can be implemented by allowing the patient to actively participate in his treatment; he then feels as if he has some control over his life. This participation may even be as minimal as having the patient report any side effects of drug or radiation therapy.

The patient generally wants to be concerned with short-range projects or goals. His future is now in terms of weeks and days rather than months and years. The nurse should help the patient to emphasize what he can still do rather than looking at deficits. He should focus on what can be accomplished day by day. This helps to decrease the patient's feelings of helplessness. The nursing staff too often tends to underestimate the influence it has on the patient's feelings about himself. Actions by the staff such as condescension, disapproval, sympathy, or depression have an effect on the patient's sense of well being. One should be more vocal in telling the patient he has done a good job, is ambulating well, is eating well, or is making progress in his daily activities. To help draw attention from the future and focus on the less threatening present, we can emphasize the importance of developing and maintaining daily routines and patterns of activity. This provides some structure to the ambiguous process of dying.

Only eleven of the 51 patients related plans for the future and with four exceptions these plans were for the near future and were concerned with spending time with the family, sitting on the porch, getting a spouse to quit smoking, and leaving the hospital. If the present is bleak and no hope exists, we can then help the patient to reminisce of the past which may lead to pleasurable reflection.

Over half of the patients interviewed expressed a feeling of isolation or loneliness (Goldfarb, 1963, p. 615). They felt others were distant and out of reach. Sometimes it appeared that patients asked for help to decrease distance by wanting to be told that they were wanted or useful. Mrs. R. said "this is worthless to waste these three drugs on me" and Mr. B. said "I am no longer good for anything and will be better off dead." They were providing the opportunity for the listener to point out positive things, to tell them that someone still cares, that they are needed, wanted, or useful. Care must be taken here to keep the response in a reality context and not make global, superficial, or false statements.

Another observation from this study was the fact that when problems seemed too overwhelming and strength was small, patients tried to gain control of situations. The patient is well aware by this time that he had no control over his disease or life span; therefore, he tries to gain control in the only ways he can. In the records of twenty patients, as their physical condition waned, the charting indicated attempts at control by refusing baths, medications, lunch, ambulation, linen changing, or treatments. In some instances the patient became quite aggressive when attempts were made to prevent him from gaining control. Nurses should not force care on the patient as long as physical comfort and safety is provided. Better still by allowing the patient to control situations such as bath times, turning, walking, and bed changes, he may accept this as enough to control and other aspects of care such as eating or medications can be carried out without refusal. One thought is that the patient may not really want control at this time but is testing to see how much control he has over his situation as his physical condition wanes. When the ambiguity of death appears to be closer, routines can also provide some stability to the patient's situation.

A direct observation from this study was the need for a patient, as he neared death, to detach himself from his surroundings—including family and friends (White, 1969, p. 881). This patient did not desire to talk; he did not want extensive care; he did not want family and friends near. One patient specifically requested no visitors. This is a time for the patient's preparation for final separation from meaningful relationships. Actions noted during this period included: the patient's appearing to be sleeping, turning his head to the wall, engaging in no conversation except possibly answering questions. Words of encouragement and reassurance have little meaning when the patient is contemplating death. The nurse's concern at this time is to let the patient know that she is there and will check on him frequently. Touch may be significant as this confirms that someone is near, shows continued support, and reassures the patient that he is not abandoned.

Nurses must help and support the family during the dying process, but special help is needed during the final stages (White, 1969, p. 687). Often the family feels that the patient is rejecting them when he wishes to be alone. Explanations and interpretations should be made and support given at this time. The nursing staff should work with the family and explain to them what is happening and how they might best help the patient. Often a simple suggestion such as sitting quietly with the patient but not talking unless he wishes to is helpful. It is important to suggest that family leave the patient periodically so both may rest. If the nurse makes this suggestion, it may help to relieve the family of guilt by allowing someone else to take the responsibility. Health personnel should help prevent the family member from making critical decisions whenever possible. At the time of death few people are objective; choices are too complex—no matter what one decides, it rarely seems best.

This study is just a beginning of the research nurses should be doing to help improve and expand their role in the health care field. The data briefly reviewed here have more specific nursing implications than we have discussed and there are other findings which were not detailed. What we have shown is that when an opportunity to verbalize was provided to the hospitalized dying patient, he did discuss his death and the information obtained during this discussion can serve as the guide for determining needed nursing action.

REFERENCES

Carson, J. Learning from a dying patient. *American Jouranl of Nursing*, 1971, 71, 333-334.
Eisman, R. Why did Joc die? *American Journal of Nursing*, 1971, 71, 501-503.
Feifel, H. (Ed.) *The meaning of death*. New York: McGraw-Hill, 1959.
Glaser, B., & Strauss, A. *Awareness of dying*. Chicago: Aldine Publishing Co., 1965.
Goldfarb, A. I. (Moderator) Death and dying: Attitudes of patient and doctor. Symposium presented at the meeting of the Group for the Advancement of Psychiatry, Asbury Park, New Jersey, April 1963.
Hoffman, E. Don't give up on me! *American Journal of Nursing*, 1971, 71, 60-62.
Kubler-Ross, E. *On death and dying*. Toronto: Macmillan, 1969.
Quint, J. C. *The nurse and the dying patient*. New York: Macmillan, 1967.
Sudnow, D. *Passing on*. Englewood Cliffs, New Jersey: Prentice-Hall, 1965.
White, L. P. (Consul. Ed.) Care of patients with fatal illness. *Annals of the New York Academy of Sciences*, 1969, 164.

CHAPTER 13

The Relationship to Death as a Source of Stress for Nurses on a Coronary Care Unit

Trevor R. Price
and
Bernard J. Bergen

Recent studies have described how intensive care settings constitute a stressful environment for nurses [1–6]. While a number of sources of stress exist, a primary source is what Hay and Oken have described as the demands imposed by the "incessant repetitive routine" of constantly monitoring patients' "vital signs" [3]. In a similar vein, Vreeland and Ellis have described the stresses imposed on nurses by the "necessity for constant intensive observation . . . " of the patient who "is incapable of control of his own physiological process" [6]. Among the stresses that this engenders are conflicting expectations that nurses be both "objective and firm" while at the same time emanating "warmth and feeling" [6]. Similarly, there are conflicting expectations that they be both ceaselessly alert in processing the incessant flow of objective data and responsive to the subjective needs of patients and their families [6].

The present study is an attempt to explore further the way in which nurses in an intensive care setting may be subjected to stressful conflicts. This study did not emerge as a function of direct observation in an intensive care setting. It emerged in the context of a request to the Department of Psychiatry by a group of nurses working in an eight bed CCU located in a teaching hospital. They requested help in setting up a discussion group for the purpose of clarifying feelings of distress they were experiencing over their work. The group was formed with the senior author as a group leader and met once a week for an hour over a period of eight months. Attendance was variable with the group size at any one time ranging from three to eight nurses. This group, similar to groups which others have described [3, 7], initially focused on a variety of highly-charged issues. What quickly assumed prominence, however, were the nurses' feelings which had first led them to ask for help in forming a discussion group. These feelings were verbalized during the course of several group sessions as feelings that things "were crazy." Almost nothing in their work environment seemed to escape this feeling: at one time or another, they verbalized the feeling that doctors were "crazy," the hospital was "crazy" and the CCU was "crazy" with the clear implication that they themselves were feeling a little "crazy."

In our attempt to understand these feelings and to help the nurses understand them, it gradually became apparent to us that one form of stress they were experiencing in the CCU had its roots in a conflict over their unconscious representation of their relationship to death. What gradually became apparent to us was that we could not understand what underlay their feelings unless we understood that, without their being fully aware of it, the signs they incessantly monitored and to which they responded not only signified the occurrence of physiological events in their patients, but unconsciously signified as well their relationship to death itself. The stress that they felt was indicative of a struggle over the meaning of this relationship. In effect, not all of the sources of stress for these nurses came from external demands made by the CCU environment; one significant source came from an internal demand that they made on themselves to experience their relationship to death as meaningful.

Relatively little attention has been given to the way in which nurses in intensive care settings actually experience the meaning of their relationship to death. Hay and Oken have noted that their "repetitive contact with death" is an "awesome addition to the burden of the nurse who has been caring for the patient and must continue to do so, knowing his outcome" [3]. They have also noted, as have others [6], the stresses imposed on nurses by the death of patients in whom they may have been emotionally invested. Our own study has convinced us that, in addition to these, nurses may also face death as a stressful ambiguity that they must make meaningful for themselves if they are to experience their own role in an intensive care setting as meaningful. Several studies have already shown that the mode in which medical caretakers experience their relationship to death informs the structure of medical care, whatever the setting, without the caretakers necessarily being conscious of it [8, 9]. The nurses in the group on which we are reporting drew our attention to the problem of experiencing a meaningful relationship to death as a source of acute inner conflict and stress.

Data from the Nurses Group

The purpose of this section is to describe the central themes that emerged from the group and to provide some illustrative material.

In the first three or four meetings the emotional conflict underlying the nurses' distress revealed itself in two conflicting themes. As we understood them, both themes expressed the nurses' feelings that the threat of death to their patients made them feel culpable. This distressing sense of culpability, however, actually seemed to be comprised of two different and conflicting feelings.

One of these feelings first expressed itself in a sense of frustration and anxiety over the organization and manner of functioning of the CCU. The nurses presented certain staffing and communication problems as the focus for their agitated discontent. These concrete problems, some of which, we found out, had already been satisfactorily resolved, proved to be the vehicle for repeatedly expressing a single question which they verbalized as, "who is in charge?; who is in control?" in the CCU. Their agitation conveyed an intense but diffuse anxiety. The anxiety was not over a failure to fulfill duties and routines for which they were responsible. It centered rather, on the problem of not letting their patients die. In effect, it seemed to stem from a sense of failing a responsibility they felt for controlling illness and death. At one point the intensity of this feeling was put into focus for the group by one of the nurses who reported an experience that she had had in the CCU. She recalled feeling that, following an unsuccessful cardio-pulmonary resuscitation effort of which she had been a part, a patient who was dying a "lingering" death had looked at her in what she had perceived to be a confused, questioning, frightened manner. This look seemed to convey to her the unspoken message that since the other patient had not been successfully resuscitated, she, the nurse, would never be able to know on whom she could count when it became her turn to face death. The report of this experience was significant not only because it expressed the group's sense of somehow failing to control death, but also because of the image which conveyed that sense of failure. In subsequent group discussions, the nurses openly expressed their feeling that their distress centered more on "lingering" patients "waiting to die" than on emergency situations that demanded immediate and urgent responses from them. In a very real sense, they were communicating that understanding stress in the CCU is a more complex matter than assessing the intensity and quantity of the external demands it makes on those who work there.

There seems reason to believe that this state of affairs may hold outside the CCU as well. Nurses in a conference on the oncology service that was being held around the same time as the CCU group and nurses observed by Wodinsky experienced similar feelings about themselves [7]. Like the nurses in the CCU, they spoke of feeling most comfortable when they could throw themselves into some demanding activity. Apparently "to be active" bore a correspondence to their sense of mastery or control over the situation and decreased their feeling of impotence.

With respect to the nurses in our group, we interpreted their "need" to be active, symbolized by their anxious preoccupation over "lingering" patients who were "waiting to die," as a need to reduce the stress of feeling that they were doing "too little" to prevent their patients from dying. This interpretation is in line with some recent data [10] which suggests that there is an apparently nearly universal feeling of helplessness in nurses who care for dying patients which seems to relate to "not being able to do more" for them. In our group, the nurses' somewhat paradoxical decrying of the occasional absence of acute emergency situations seemed to express the relative lack of opportunities for them to escape a self-consciousness that aroused distressing feelings about their capacity to meet the demands for absolute control that they felt death imposed on them.

At the same time, almost from the beginning, a conflicting feeling that they were doing "too much" for their patients was interwoven with their feeling of doing "too little" for them. Side by side with the feeling of being culpable for not "knowing what to do" or "how to act" in order to reverse a particular patient's inevitable course toward death — an accusation they frequently directed toward the physician in charge — they also felt that what they did do to keep a patient alive, as they phrased it, often "prevented nature from taking its course."

This feeling of being culpable for doing "too much" for their patients emerged around two themes. One nurse reported that for her, "patients during an arrest often seemed to become a part of the machinery." The group discussion of this theme seems best summarized by what Hay and Oken characterized as "multiple threats to the stability of (the nurse's) body boundaries, her sense of self and her feelings of humanity and reality" [3]. One of the ways that nurses in our group struggled with their perceptions that the "other worldly" technological trappings of the CCU violated some crucial aspect of their patient's humanity was to focus their angry feelings on the doctors. The group's angry mood was captured by the theme that the doctors were playing a false role in the CCU. As one nurse inaccurately but bitterly put it: "CCU's haven't lowered MI death rates." The nurses perceived the doctors as often hiding "weakness" and impotence behind a blind insistence on "pouring it on" or continuing to "pull out all the stops" in the face of what they (the nurses) verbalized as unavoidable and, in fact, sometimes desireable death for some of the "lingering" patients.

In one sense, we could say that the interwoven themes of doing "too little" and "too much" for their patients expressed the nurses' preoccupation over the ethical problem of prolonging life that is so much in the public view today. They did not, however, experience it as such. They experienced the problem, rather, as involving the need to construct a relationship with death in an environment where the very routine of work confronted them with death's ubiquitous presence. In the face of this confrontation with death, the ethical abstractions of the problem of prolonging life were experienced by the nurses as an intimate problem of making sense of the image of themselves as agents who bear a responsibility for no less than the control of death.

The problem of their conflicted feelings about themselves as being responsible for the control of death surfaced with little difficulty in the course of the group discussions. In fact, it had really been there from the onset.

In the early group sessions the nurses had verbalized those conflicted feelings by talking about elements of their CCU training. One group member stated that their training started with an admonition from their instructor that "any patient in the unit can fibrillate (arrest) at any time." She expressed this in a way that made it almost unmistakeable that she and the other nurses all felt that they had been trained not only to be responsible for detecting and responding to such an event swiftly and effectively, but also that in some ill-defined and unrealistic sense, they were or could be held responsible for the actual occurrence of the event itself. Their distress was essentially a struggle to come to grips with this ambiguity. The intensity of this struggle was expressed at another time in terms of an anecdote told by another of the nurses. She described how an admired former CCU nurse friend of hers had verbalized some of her internal conflicts and thereby came to find the CCU a more enjoyable, tolerable and less-stressful place to work. As she reported it, her friend, faced with the demands made by a great number of critically-ill patients and potential deaths, stopped in the middle of the CCU one day, nearly paralyzed with a combination of fear, frustration and overwhelming external stimuli. Reflecting on what she had until then unrealistically and irrationally perceived as her nursing function and role in the CCU, to contain, control, and even defeat death, she said to herself, "You know the worst thing that might happen is that a patient might die." The group member reported that her friend upon saying that, felt a sense of relief and with renewed determination was able to continue to do what she realistically could, albeit not all that she might have previously expected of herself. It was clearly an anecdote directed at the groups own inability to accept the inevitability of death at some level of their experience.

No doubt this inability expresses deep psychological wishes. For the nurses in the group it also expressed their immediate problem of coming to grips with the limits of their responsibility for the control of death. The signs that they constantly monitored in the CCU not only pointed to physiological events in their patients, but were also, for them, the signs by which death itself announced its presence as something they must control and prevent. At the same time, the nurses seemed to have no clear concept of the limits of such a possibility. Although they could not deny their limited capacity to control death, this did not necessarily signify for them that they had a limited responsibility for such control. Unconsciously, the boundary was blurred between their awareness of *being* responsible for the care of an ill or dying patient and their *feeling* of being responsible for the occurrence of the patient's illness or death. This latter feeling informed their awareness of the former. Thus unconscious blurring of the boundary between the two made them unable to define an acceptable and meaningful image of themselves in relationship to death.

This difficulty over making sense of their relationship to death was captured by a particular metaphor. In one group session, one of the nurses capped off a discussion of the "false" role of doctors played in the CCU, by observing, with some anger, that doctors in the CCU were "both God and not God at the same time." Regardless of the extent to which this may or may not reflect a generally accurate perception of doctors, it clearly seemed to reflect the nurses' own fundamental confusion over their own relationship to death. In effect, the metaphor of being "both God and not God at the same time" seemed to express their own conflict over being agents who bear a responsibility for the control of death.

Our overall formulation of what underlay the nurses' distress is, of course, our way of attempting to grasp their experience rather than their own way of verbalizing it. However, a critical point in the group process came when the issue of the limits of the possibility of controlling death surfaced for full and open discussion.

After this issue was directly discussed for a brief time, the nurses took the initiative to move the discussion away from the problem of the control of death as such and focus it on more matter-of-fact problems raised by instances of "disruptive" acting out behavior on the part of patients in general. One such discussion, for example, took up the problem of the occasional sexual pass that patients make at nurses. As we interpret it, the nurses were "defusing" the intensity of coming to grips with the limits of their responsibility for their dying patients by displacing the issue onto behavior problems for which they had no intense feelings of responsibility or culpability.

Undoubtedly, the timing of the nurses' shift in focus away from the issue of their relationship to death was influenced by different factors on the level of group process. Whatever may have influenced the timing of this shift, their ability to explore the question of responsibility in general terms did prove to be significant. Toward the end of the group they returned to the issue of the limits of their responsibility for controlling death. When they returned to the issue they did so in a manner that openly confronted it. They openly spoke about having conflicted feelings over being responsible and culpable for the illness and death of their patients. In other words, at the end of the group they were able to see something of their conflict over the image of themselves as being responsible for the control of death. Not surprisingly, this does not mean that they were able to resolve the conflict. They continued to express feelings of despair and, at times, agitated feelings of helplessness over finding a meaningful way to relate to death. In effect, the limits of their capacity to control death and the feelings of being responsible for the very occurrence of death itself remained a source of conflict; but they were able to address their feelings about this issue more clearly than before. At the very least, as one nurse put it, toward the end of the group they felt "less crazy" then they had at the outset.

Discussion

It is our contention that the problem from which the nurses suffered—the unconscious blurring of the boundary between an awareness of being responsible for the care of an ill or dying patient and the feeling of being responsible for the occurrence of the patient's illness or death — is not a kind of pathology or "hangup" that necessarily requires psychiatric attention. We feel that the stress which they experienced is endemic in our time, both in and out of medicine. The problem, for reasons that are not clear to us, had surfaced for the nurses at a time when they felt motivated to ask for help from a department of psychiatry. However, this does not make it a psychiatric problem in a medical sense. From the point of view of the nurses in the group, we see it as a problem that reflects a concatenation of at least two forces.

On the one hand, it seems reasonable to assume that their feelings of being responsible for the occurrence of the illness or death of their patients reflects the pressures of internal needs. One of these, we feel, is the well-known and frequently discussed "need" to deny the fact of one's own ultimate death. The need to deny one's death seems to manifest itself in more complicated maneuvers than simply shutting off one's awareness of death itself. It may involve a need to pay attention to death — to develop an active relationship toward it — in which one feels unconsciously responsible for the event of death so that one can eventually control it and, possibly, eliminate it from the world. Indeed, we feel that this maneuver under the pressure of the need to deny one's own ultimate death underlies Phillipe Aries' penetrating observation that in the "normal existence" of our time, death "no longer has any positive meaning at all. It is merely the negative side of what we really see, what we really know, and what we really feel" [11]. To throw ourselves into accenting what we assumed to be the "real" and the "positive" in life, carries with it the responsibility for eliminating the negative. In this respect, Aries' observation is significant that embalming, which in former ages was "intended primarily to impart something of the incorruptibility of the saints to the dead," has become "in modern America chemical techniques for preserving the body (in order to) make us forget death by creating an illusion of life" [12]. No doubt, when we assume responsibility for the occurrence of the event of death, we only succeed in being embarrassed over its ubiquitous presence. Apparently, however, being confronted by the limits of the possibility of controlling death doesn't prevent us from harboring the unconscious feeling of being responsible for its occurrence. It is as if we believe that to give up this unconscious feeling would result in our becoming a hostage to the freedom of death at every moment of our life. This may or may not be so, but apparently we are reluctant to face the anxiety of trying to find out.

The structure and values of the institution of medicine, in our view, are strongly involved in reinforcing such an unconscious feeling. In fact, the structure and values of medicine may reflect, in part, its status as a critical instrument that society uses in pursuit of the project of controlling and eliminating death. With respect to the nurses in our group, this may be the second pressure that was reflected in their own troublesome unconscious feelings. Hay and Oken have noted that intensive care settings project a kind of "surrealistic" atmosphere [3]. For the nurses in our group, this seemed to be conveyed not only by the sounds of the patients and the sight of the apparatus in the CCU, but by what the image of the CCU as a whole conveyed about the potentially unlimited capacity of humans to control and eliminate death. This implicit image of the CCU, left unaddressed, seemed to be a factor in keeping the boundary blurred for the nurses, between their awareness of being responsible for caring for their patients, and their feelings of being responsible for the life-threatening events that happened to their patients that might terminate their lives.

It is hard not to conclude that the image conveyed by the CCU reflects an unspoken wish for the unlimited possibility of controlling death that is pervasive in medicine in general. Certainly the general trait of a need for "control" seems to be endemic in physicians. Balint has even characterized the doctor's role in the doctor-patient relationship as that of fulfilling an "apostolic function"—the conversion of the heathen [13]. Marmor has suggested that many physicians experience irrational and unrealistic feelings of power, superiority and control as the result of a constant exercise of authority [14]. In general, the belief system in medicine seems to have as its main tenet that medical science both can and should seek mastery over all medical problems such that illness and death are continually put in retreat. What is rarely discussed and left ambiguous is the scope of the battle, and the strength of the enemy's forces that place limits on the size of the possible victory. This unspoken ambiguity may not be unrelated to either Burton's data that show that psychotherapists have an "extraordinary and covert" sensitivity to death [15], or to Feifel's data that show that physicians have a greater fear of death than non-physicians [16]. Feifel suggests that one function of medicine for physicians may be to control personal concerns about illness and death by acquiring mastery over disease through the acquisition of medical knowledge and skills. It is the unpredicted death, as Sudnow [9] and Siegler [17] point out, that provokes the most discomfort in both doctors and nurses. This discomfort is not only over an anxiety that somehow they may have been negligent in the care of the patient, but also because somehow such a death confronts them with an unacceptable image of themselves as a failure.

For us, our experience with the nurses in the discussion group raises the question of the toll that an unconscious feeling of being responsible for the occurrence of death can take on both medical caretakers and their patients. It is not that the clarification of such feelings can resolve the issue of constructing a meaningful relationship to death. Clarifying feelings can never supply an answer to the question of what is meaningful. It can only supply an opportunity to take a chance on finding something more meaningful than before. This chance, in medicine, concerns not only the possibility of making the demands of the intensive care environment more tolerable for nurses and others, but of improving the overall care of the dying patient. As long as we harbor unconscious feelings of being responsible for the occurrence of the illness and death of the patient, it will be hard for us not to see death as the kind of embarrassing scandal that leads us to isolate and otherwise violate the personhood of the dying patient. Unfortunately, if our particular experience with nurses on the CCU has any generality, then it would appear that the question of constructing a meaningful relationship to death still remains largely under the taboo of silence in medicine as in society.

REFERENCES

1. L. F. Bishop and P. Reichert, The Psychological Impact of the Coronary Care Unit, *Psychosomatics, 10,* pp. 189-192, May-June, 1969.
2. J. E. D. Gardam, Nursing Stresses in the Intensive Care Unit, Letter to the Editor, *JAMA, 208,* pp. 2337-2338, June 23, 1969.
3. D. Hay and D. Oken, The Psychological Stresses of Intensive Care Unit Nursing, *Psychosomatic Medicine, 34,* pp. 109-118, Mar.-Apr., 1972.
4. D. S. Kornfeld, Psychiatric Problems in an Intensive Care Unit, *Medical Clinics of North America, 55,* pp. 1353-1363, Sept. 1971.
5. D. S. Kornfeld, Psychiatric View of the Intensive Care Unit, *British Medical Journal, 1,* pp. 108-110, Jan., 1969.
6. R. Vreeland and G. L. Ellis, Stresses on the Nurse in an Intensive Care Unit, *JAMA, 208,* pp. 332-334, Apr., 1969.
7. A. Wodinsky, Psychiatric Consultation with Nurses on a Leukemia Service, *Mental Hygiene, 48,* pp. 282-287, 1964.
8. B. G. Glaser and A. L. Strauss, *Awareness of Dying,* Aldine Press, Chicago, 1965.
9. D. Sudnow, *Passing On: The Social Organization of Dying,* Prentice Hall, Englewood Cliffs, N. J., 1967.
10. Editorial Report, Results of a Research Questionnaire on Death and Dying, distributed to 15,430 nurses, *Nursing, 75,* pp. 16-24, 1975.
11. P. Aries, Death Inside Out, *Hastings Center Studies, 2,* pp. 3-18, May, 1974.

12. P. Aries, *Western Attitudes Toward Death: From the Middle Ages to the Present*, Johns Hopkins University Press, Baltimore, 1974.
13. M. Balint, *The Doctor, His Patient, And the Illness*, International Universities Press, N. Y., 1957.
14. J. Marmor, The Feeling of Superiority: An Occupational Hazard in the Practice of Psychotherapy, *American Journal of Psychiatry, 110*, pp. 370-376, Nov., 1953.
15. A. Burton, Death as a Counter Transference, *Psychoanalysis and the Psychoanalytic Review, 49*, pp. 3-20, 1962.
16. H. Feifel, S. Hanson, R. Jones, and L. Edwards, Physicians Consider Death, *Proceedings, 75th Annual Convention of the APA*, pp. 201-202, 1967.
17. M. Siegler, Pascal's Wager and the Hanging of Crepe, *New England Journal of Medicine, 293*, pp. 853-857, Oct., 1975.

CHAPTER 14

How the Medical Staff Copes with Dying Patients: A Critical Review*

Richard Schulz
and
David Aderman

This paper examines the attitudes and resultant behavior which typically characterize the interaction between medical practitioners and the dying patient. The focus will not only be on how doctors and nurses regard death and the dying, but also on the dying patient's feelings about his impending death and the treatment he receives from the medical staff. The aim is to gain some understanding of the plight of the dying patient, to learn whether he is informed of his condition, and to determine how he is treated by the medical staff.

Attitudes and Behavior of Physicians

Numerous researchers have observed that physicians avoid a patient once he begins to die [1-4]. To explain this avoidance behavior, researchers have focused either on the physician's training or his personality. Those investigators who are of the opinion that a basic personality structure is responsible for the physician's behavior toward the dying, speculate that individuals who become physicians do so because of their inordinate fear of death. Becoming a physician, then, has been interpreted as an attempt to master death [5-7]. Kasper agreed with this point of view [8], and added that "part of the psychological motivation of the physician is to cure himself and live forever; he wishes to be a scientist in order to gain mastery over life by treating people as things" [1].

* Preparation of this report was facilitated by Grant GS-35175 from the National Science Foundation to the second author.

Although not conclusive, some empirical support for self-selection on the basis of personality is found in a study of medical students by Livingston and Zimet [1]. These investigators reasoned that medical students high in authoritarianism would be "better defended" against unconscious fears and therefore have less overt death anxiety. As a result, these students would function comfortably in specialities where death is relatively common (e.g., surgery). Students low on authoritarianism, on the other hand, would be aware of and made uncomfortable by their death anxiety and as a result choose specialities where death is an uncommon occurrence (e.g., psychiatry). The results supported their hypothesis: Psychiatrically oriented students were less authoritarian and showed higher death anxiety than students oriented toward surgery. The fact that this was true regardless of year of training seems to indicate that medical students decide on a specialty upon entering medical school and that this decision is in part determined by their personality structure.

These personality structures are undoubtedly reinforced by medical training which emphasizes an interaction style between physician and patient described by Lief and Fox as "detached concern" [9]. The medical student is advised to be empathic and involved with the patient, but above all, to remain objective. In addition, the specifics of medical training are usually focused at saving lives to the exclusion of dealing with patients who are defined as terminal. As a consequence of both their personality structures and the training they receive, physicians may associate dying patients with failure and disappointment. A patient's death challenges the physician's ability as a healer and sensitizes him to the temporal limits of his own life. It is not surprising, then, that physicians may tend to avoid patients in the process of dying.

Perhaps the most important decision the physician makes when his patient becomes terminal is whether or not to tell the patient about his condition. There already exists a large body of literature advising the physician on this question [2, 3, 10-15], but only a few researchers have actually attempted to determine the extent to which this advice is followed [12, 16].

In an editorial directed at physicians, Lasagna advised physicians not to lie about the terminal patient's condition [13]. He also recommended that relatives of the patient should be forewarned. Lirette et al. similarly advised letting the patient know his condition but caution the physician to tell the patient gradually [14]. Noyes pointed out that the physician holds the key to providing the patient with a good death, and this is best accomplished by informing the patient of his condition [10]. Kübler-Ross focused on the requirements of a "good" death and stressed the physician's role in fulfilling these requirements [2]. Through intimate interaction, she argued, the physician can help the patient reach a calm acceptance of his death. Wahl agreed with Kübler-Ross that the physician should acquire intimate knowledge of the patient, but at the same time he cautioned the physician to be selective in choosing those patients to be informed of their condition [11]. Although not telling a patient may deprive him of the opportunity for sympathetic communication with physicians and friends, there are some individuals who are too afraid of death to face such information. Those patients who are told, Wahl stresses, should never be told in such a way as to rob them of all hope: "The patient should never be left with the feeling that the physician has played his last card and that nothing further can be done" [11]. Evidence supporting the conclusion that patients should be told their condition was reported by Glaser and Strauss [3]. After several years of observing patients and medical staff, they found that most patients learned of their condition from cues given by medical personnel, even when they were not specifically told their condition. These cues ranged in subtlety from facial expressions and avoidance behavior to discussions of the patient's condition in front of the patient.

A number of practitioners have addressed themselves specifically to the question of whether or not to tell terminal *cancer* patients of their condition [17-21]. Here again, the consensus position is that it is best to be truthful but gentle. Litin argued that it is a patient's legal right to know the truth [17]. In Hoerr's opinion, honesty is always the best policy in the long run [18]. Desjardins, Wyrsch, and Oken all advocated a "play it by ear" policy. In most cases a patient should be told, they advised, but one should let the patient be the guide as to how much and in what way the information is to be conveyed [19-21].

It should be noted that with only few exceptions, the advice given above comes from medical practitioners, primarily doctors, and is therefore directed at colleagues. One would expect then that medical doctors would be likely to adhere to such advice. The evidence on the behavior of physicians indicates, however, that this is not the case. Fitts and Ravdin found that of four hundred and forty-two physicians sampled by a mail survey in the Philadelphia area, over two-thirds reported that they infrequently or never disclosed the diagnosis of terminal cancer [16]. A similar nationwide mail survey of over four thousand physicians revealed that 22 per cent never told while 62 per cent sometimes informed the patient of incurable cancer [22]. In a recent study reported by Caldwell and Mishara seventy-three medical doctors at a large metropolitan Detroit, Michigan, private hospital were asked to participate in a research project on the attitudes and feelings of medical doctors [32]. Although the majority of physicians consented to participate when originally approached, sixty of the seventy-three doctors refused to complete the interview once they found out the questions dealt with their attitudes toward dying patients. All of the thirteen doctors who completed the interview agreed that the dying patient has the right to know that his diagnosis is terminal, but only two of those thirteen admitted to actually telling their patients of a terminal diagnosis. This inconsistency between attitude and behavior may reflect the fact that physicians find the task of actually informing the patient psychologically too difficult for them and/or not their responsibility.

In a more comprehensive study, Oken endeavored to find out not only how physicians behave in regard to informing the cancer patient but also to discover what reasons they gave for their behavior [12]. Oken sent a questionnaire to two hundred and nineteen members of the medical staff of Michael Reese Hospital, a private nonprofit teaching hospital in Chicago. Ninety-five per cent of the questionnaires were returned and 30 per cent of those cooperating were subsequently interviewed. Consistent with previous findings, about 90 per cent of Oken's respondents indicated that they did not tell patients their diagnosis. Those that did tell were found to employ euphemisms for incurable cancer such as "growth," "hyperplastic tissue," "lesion," "mass," or "tumor." The primary reason offered for telling those few patients who were told was concern for the patient's financial responsibility. That is, physicians thought it important for some patients to have the opportunity for planning their financial affairs. Primarily emotional reasons were given for not telling the patient: "Knowledge of cancer is a death sentence, A Buchenwald, a torture"; "the cruelest thing in the world"; "like hitting the patient with a baseball bat" [12].

Oken attempted to find out where physicians acquired their policies of not telling. Only 5 per cent mentioned medical school or hospital training as the major source whereas the great majority, 77 per cent, listed clinical experience. Oken reasoned that if experience did indeed determine the physician's policy, then young doctors should have listed experience less frequently as a determinant of their policy; however, young doctors were just as likely as old doctors to list experience as the determinant of their policy. Oken concluded that the physicians' claim that their policy is based on experience was far from accurate. Further probing showed that more often than not a physician's policy was based on "opinion, belief, and conviction, heavily weighted with emotional justification" and not on critical observation [12].

Oken's respondents also voiced substantial opposition to the idea of changing their policy on informing patients. Eighty per cent felt that policy change in the future was unlikely although over half felt that they could be swayed by research. A sizeable minority stated that they "wouldn't believe it, or 'it couldn't be true,' if research suggested a policy different from their own" [12]. Ten per cent of the group objected even to the suggestion that research be carried out in this area.

Attitude and Behavior of Nurses

Although the literature on medical staff other than physicians is sparse, some data on the behavior of nurses toward the dying is available. A study similar to Oken's was carried out by Pearlman, Stotsky, and Bernard [23]. These investigators interviewed sixty-eight nursing personnel in a variety of institutions, from state hospitals to nursing homes, and found that those nurses having more experience with death were more likely to avoid the dying and felt more uneasy discussing death with dying patients than less experienced nurses. Lawrence LeShan (reported by Kastenbaum and Aisenberg [4]) recorded nurses' avoidance of terminal patients. Using a stop watch, LeShan measured how long it took nurses to respond to bedside calls and found that it took them significantly more time to respond to terminal patients than to less severely ill patients. Apparently, experienced nurses had learned to cope with death by avoiding or denying it, a behavioral pattern not unlike the one found among physicians. Like the physicians in Oken's study, the experienced nurses also advocated experience with dying patients as the best means for learning how to deal with them. The less experienced nurses, on the other hand, stressed the need for courses and seminars on managing the dying patient as the best means for learning how to deal with death.

What do nurses tell a patient when directly confronted by his thoughts on death? Kastenbaum tried to answer this question by asking two hundred attendants and nurses at a geriatric hospital how they responded to patients' statements about death (e.g., "I think I'm going to die soon," or "I wish I could just end it all") [24]. Kastenbaum found five general categories of responses.

RESPONSES TO PATIENTS' DEATH STATEMENTS

Reassurance—"You're doing so well now. You don't have to feel this way."

Denial—"You don't really mean that . . . You're not going to die. Oh, you're going to live to be a hundred."

Changing the subject—"Let's think of something more cheerful. You shouldn't say things like that; there are better things to talk about."

Fatalism—"We are all going to die sometime, and it's a good thing we don't know when. When God wants you, He will take you."

Discussion—"What makes you feel that way today? Is it something that happened, something somebody said?"

The most popular response was some form of avoidance, either fatalism, denial, or changing the subject. The majority, 82 per cent, evaded any discussion of the patient's thoughts or feelings. "The clear tendency was to 'turn off' the patient as quickly and deftly as possible" [24]. Two reasons were given for this behavior. One, nurses wanted to make the patient happy, and felt that the best way to do this was to get him to think about something else. Two, nurses wanted to protect themselves. Most admitted feeling very uncomfortable talking about death, saying that it "bugged" them or "shook them up" to talk about it.

The inability of nurses to deal with the dying patient is also documented in Jeanne C. Quint's book, *The Nurse and the Dying Patient* [25]. She analyzed the training that nurses receive which could bring about this avoidance behavior and concluded that because the young nurse is made to feel very concerned about making mistakes she learns to defend herself by concentrating on routines and rituals that tend to alienate her from the patient she is caring for. The solution, of course, is to provide professional training early in the nurse's career that will enable her to adequately handle the dying patient.

It should be apparent now that there is a great disparity between the advice offered by some practitioners regarding the treatment of terminal patients and the behavior of most physicians and nurses. The next section examines the terminal patient's feelings about how he is treated by the medical staff and the consequences of such treatment for his psychological well-being.

Patients' Desire for Information About Their Illness

Kübler-Ross and Glaser and Strauss argue that the terminal patient acquires information about his condition even if not directly informed. Data presented below tends to refute this [2, 3]. A sizeable proportion of terminal patients appear to remain unaware of their condition until the end, although it is sometimes difficult to separate what the patient knows from what he is willing to accept. Most patients are probably best classified as being in a condition of uncertain certainty that Avery Weisman has called "middle knowledge" [4]. That is, dying patients are at some level aware that they will not recover, but they vacillate between knowing and not knowing this.

Although few researchers have attempted to specifically determine how aware the dying patient is of his condition, research on the patient's attitude toward the medical staff and the treatment he receives is more abundant. In his study of healthy nonpatients, psychiatric patients, somatically ill patients, and the dying, Cappon asked each group whether or not they would like to know if a serious illness was terminal [26]. The majority of subjects, regardless of medical status, responded, yes. Of the four groups, however, dying patients desired this information least (67 per cent). Eighty-one per cent of the somatic patients desired such information, while 82 per cent of the psychiatric patients and 91 per cent of the nonpatients said they would like to know if a serious illness was terminal. Dying patients were also less interested than the other groups in information revealing "when he will die" and "how he will feel on dying."

Cappon concluded from his findings that physicians should be cautious and not give more information than is wanted. Apparently unaware of the literature showing that physicians only rarely inform the patient of his condition, he advised that physicians, as nonpatients, should recognize that "what they think *now* they themselves would want to know may not hold later when they become ill" [26].

It is unfortunate that in his study Cappon did not report data on whether or not the dying patients knew their condition was terminal when they filled out his questionnaire. One might expect different attitudes toward death and varying desires for information as a function of such knowledge. It could be that Cappon's dying patients were less curious about what it's like to die because they already knew. Hinton's work in part addresses itself to this question [27].

Hinton and his collaborators repeatedly interviewed two groups of patients residing in the same hospital. One group of one hundred and twenty-one patients was selected on the basis that they had a fatal illness, with death expected within six months. A second group consisted of matched controls. These patients entered the hospital at the same time that dying patients did, were the same age, had an illness affecting the same system, and were under the same physician's care. A control patient was always interviewed on the same day as the dying patient. The structure of the interview was left open to the interviewer, provided he collected information on age, sex, marital status, social class, strength of religiosity, level of physical distress, depression, anxiety, and the patient's awareness of dying. Where possible, patients' responses were systematically categorized and analyzed using a chi-square analysis.

Since control patients did not differ from dying patients on any of the demographic variables (e.g., sex, age, social class, etc.), Hinton felt justified in attributing differences on the psychological variables to degree of illness. A cursory analysis showed that physical distress as measured by pain, dyspnoea (difficulty in breathing), nausea, malaise or cough was greater for the dying patients than the nondying controls. This is hardly surprising given that dying patients were physically more deteriorated. Dying patients were also significantly more depressed and anxious and were, of course, much more likely to perceive themselves as terminal than nondying patients.

Looking at relationships between dependent measures, Hinton found that awareness of the possibility of death was significantly related to a mood of depression. Over 60 per cent of the dying patients who showed awareness of death expressed mild or moderate depression. These same individuals were, however, not significantly more anxious, although the results were in that direction. Awareness was also related to greater physical distress and longer illness.

Depression and anxiety were both related to religious faith, but not in the same way. Those with strong religious beliefs showed the least amount of anxiety but the most depression, while individuals with no religious faith were least depressed and only slightly more anxious than strong faith individuals. Patients with some Christian beliefs were high on both anxiety and depression. Perhaps these patients were anxious about their lack of faith and at the same time depressed in the realization that religion really had little to offer. Hinton was unable to offer an explanation for these results or for most of his other findings. His use of univariate instead of multivariate analysis methods undoubtedly hindered his explanatory efforts.

Both Hinton and Cappon concluded that the dying patient is better off not informed about his condition. Thirty-three per cent of Cappon's dying subjects expressed a desire not to be told, while Hinton showed that dying patients aware of their condition were more depressed and slightly more anxious than nondying patients. Neither study is, however, convincing in its conclusion. Cappon, for instance, based his conclusion on the fact that fewer dying than nondying patients desired information about terminal illness. Yet well over half (67 per cent) still wanted to know. In addition, Cappon did not report whether these responses came from dying patients who already knew they were dying or from patients who perhaps only suspected it but were afraid to find out. In any case, the conclusion that dying patients more often than not desire information about their condition is better justified by the data than the conclusion offered by Cappon.

Hinton can be criticized on similar grounds. He assumed a causal relationship between awareness of condition and depression. His basic argument was that knowledge of condition leads to depression which is undesirable; therefore, patients should not be informed. His data also showed, however, that depression was significantly higher in those patients who had endured longer illnesses and greater physical distress. Furthermore, as was indicated earlier, awareness of dying came more often to those who had greater physical distress and longer illnesses. Thus, awareness, depression, physical distress, and longer illness were all positively related in dying patients. Given these relationships one can just as logically argue that physical distress or longer illness result in depression and awareness of dying; or, perhaps even that depression results in longer illness, greater physical distress and awareness of dying. Many reasonable causal chains are possible and none can be definitively ruled out given the data presented in this study. Fortunately other data on this issue are available.

Kelly and Friesen found that of one hundred cancer patients eighty-nine favored knowing their diagnosis [28]. One hundred clinic patients who did not have cancer were asked if they would like to know the results of an examination that revealed cancer, and the great majority (82 per cent) said, yes. Similar results are reported by Samp and Curerri who surveyed five hundred and sixty cancer patients and their families and found that 87 per cent felt that a patient should be told [29]. Subjects who had cancer in these studies were aware of their diagnosis before these surveys were taken. These results are, therefore, slightly suspect since "patients cannot permit doubts about the wisdom of the policy of those whom they need to trust so desperately" [12].

In a recent interview study, K. A. Achte, a Finnish psychiatrist, focused on how one hundred cancer patients acquired the information that they had terminal cancer [30]. Forty of the patients had been spontaneously told of their condition. Twenty-nine had asked for a diagnosis and received a frank answer, and thirty-one were reluctant to find out anything about their condition, although six of these patients suspected it was cancer. The majority of the patients (85 per cent) had suffered from intense anxiety and depression upon learning the true nature of their illness, but in most cases these symptoms dissipated in a short time.

None of the patients who were spontaneously informed were critical of the act of informing, but a small number did criticize the manner in which they were told, describing the physicians' behavior as tactless and insensitive. Patients who had inquired about their diagnosis were most favorable toward physicians. The remaining patients avoided all discussion of the disease with the interviewer.

This study, then, lends support to the position that the majority of patients desire to be told and suffer no permanent negative consequences as a result of being informed of their condition. It should be noted, however, that subjects who were informed were not randomly selected. This self-selection process may have attenuated the potential negative effects of informing individuals of their condition. The crucial study, where subjects are randomly assigned to information or no information condition, has not been carried out. The dependent measures in such a study would include blind assessment of psychological and physical well-being of the patient.

Conclusion

Alban Wheeler has argued that the dying person is a deviant in the medical subculture [31]. Much of the research reviewed above supports this view. The dying person elicits aversive attitudes from his audience and these attitudes often result in avoidance behaviors on the part of physicians and nurses. Future research should be aimed at further documenting medical staff interactions with dying patients as well as investigating ways in which attitudes of practitioners might be changed, should that be necessary. One possible approach to changing the attitudes of practitioners might be to convince medical and nursing schools to focus on the social-psychological aspects of death and dying as part of their curriculum.

With the increased availability of reports such as this, it is hoped that social-psychological aspects of medical practice will become an important part of the education of medical practitioners.

REFERENCES

1. P. B. Livingston and C. N. Zimet, Death Anxiety, Authoritarianism and Choice of Specialty in Medical Students, *Journal Nervous Mental Disease*, *140*, pp. 222-230, 1965.
2. E. Kübler-Ross, *On Death and Dying*, Macmillan, New York, 1964.
3. B. G. Glaser and A. L. Strauss, *Awareness of Dying*, Aldine, Chicago, 1965.
4. R. Kastenbaum and R. Aisenberg, *The Psychology of Death*, Springer, New York, 1972.
5. C. W. Wahl, The Physician's Management of the Dying Patient, in J. Masserman, (ed.), *Current Psychiatric Therapies*, Grune and Stratton, New York, 1962.
6. H. Feifel and J. Heller, Normalcy, Illness and Death, Proceedings of the Third World Congress of Psychiatry, University of Toronto Press, Toronto, 1960.
7. H. Feifel, S. Hanson and R. Jones, Physicians Consider Death, Proceedings of the 75th Annual Convention of the American Psychological Association, *2*, pp. 201-202, 1967.
8. A. M. Kasper, The Doctor and Death, in H. Feifel, (ed.), *The Meaning of Death*, McGraw Hill, New York, 1959.
9. H. I. Lief and R. C. Fox, Training for "Detached Concern" in Medical Students, in H. I. Lief and N. R. Lief, (eds.), *The Psychological Basis of Medical Practice*, Harper and Row, New York, 1963.
10. R. Noyes, Jr., The Art of Dying, *Perspectives in Biological Medicine*, *14*, pp. 432-447, 1971.
11. C. W. Wahl, Should a Patient Be Told the Truth?, in A. H. Kutcher, (ed.), *But Not to Lose*, Fredrick Fell, New York, pp. 104-107, 1969.
12. D. Oken, What to Tell Cancer Patients, *Journal American Medical Association*, *175*, pp. 86-94, 1961.
13. L. Lasagna, The Doctor and the Dying Patient, *Journal Chronic Disease*, *22*, pp. 65-68, 1969.
14. W. L. Lirette, R. L. Palmer, I. D. Ibarra, et al., Management of Patients With Terminal Cancer, *Postgraduate Medicine*, *46*, pp. 145-149, 1969.
15. The Doctor and the Dying Patient, R. H. David, (ed.), *Symposium on the Doctor and the Dying Patient*, University of Southern California School of Medicine Postgraduate Division of the Department of Psychiatry and Gerontology Center, 1971.
16. W. T. Fitts and I. S. Ravdin, What Philadelphia Physicians Tell Patients With Cancer, *Journal American Medical Association*, *153*, pp. 901-904, 1953.
17. E. M. Litin, What Shall We Tell the Cancer Patient?, a psychiatrist's view, *Proceedings of Mayo Clinic*, *35*, pp. 247-250, 1960.
18. S. O. Hoerr, Thoughts on What to Tell the Patient With Cancer, *Cleveland Clinic Quarterly*, *30*, pp. 11-16, 1963.
19. A. V. Desjardins, What the Physician Should Tell a Patient Who is Affected With a Malignant Lesion, *Journal Main Medical Association*, *30*, pp. 16-17, 1960.
20. J. Wyrsh, Should We Inform the Patient About the Cancer Diagnosis? *Schweiz Medizinische Wochenschrift*, *92*, pp. 1577-1588, 1962.

21. D. Oken, The Physician, The Patient, and Cancer, *Illinois Medical Journal*, *120*, pp. 333-334, 1961.
22. D. Rennick, What Should Physicians Tell Cancer Patients?, *New Medical Materia*, *2*, pp. 51-53, 1960.
23. J. Pearlman, B. A. Stotsky and J. R. Dominick, Attitudes Toward Death Among Nursing Home Personnel, *Journal Genetic Psychology*, *114*, pp. 63-75, 1969.
24. R. Kastenbaum, Multiple Perspectives on a Geriatric "Death Valley," *Community Mental Health Journal*, *3*, pp. 21-29, 1967.
25. J. C. Quint, *The Nurse and the Dying Patient*, Aldine, Chicago, 1967.
26. D. Cappon, Attitudes Of and Toward the Dying, *Canadian Medical Association Journal*, *87*, pp. 693-700, 1969.
27. J. M. Hinton, The Physical and Mental Distress of the Dying, *Quarterly Journal of Medicine*, *32*, pp. 1-21, 1963.
28. W. D. Kelly and S. R. Friesen, Do Cancer Patients Want to be Told?, *Surgery*, *27*, pp. 822-826, 1950.
29. R. J. Samp and A. R. Curreri, Questionnaire Survey on Public Cancer Education Obtained from Cancer Patients and Their Families, *Cancer*, *10*, pp. 382-384, 1957.
30. K. A. Achte and M. L. Vauhkonen, Cancer and the Psyche, *Omega*, *2*, pp. 45-56, 1971.
31. A. L. Wheeler, The Dying Person: A Deviant in the Medical Subculture. Paper presented at the annual meeting of the Southern Sociological Society, Atlanta, Georgia, April, 1973.
32. D. Caldwell and B. L. Mishara, Research on Attitudes of Medical Doctors Toward the Dying Patient: A Methodological Problem, *Omega*, *3*, pp. 341-346, 1972.

CHAPTER
15

Attitudes of Physicians
on Disclosing Information to
and Maintaining Life
for Terminal Patients

Raymond G. Carey
and
Emil J. Posavac

Since Kübler-Ross and others have been reporting on dying patients,
physicians have been under increasing criticism for allegedly failing to be open
and honest with terminal patients under their care [1]. For example, Schulz
and Aderman in a review of the literature concluded that the majority of
physicians adhere to a policy of not sharing their diagnosis with the dying
patient [2]. To support this conclusion they cite four studies that were
conducted some years ago. Fitts and Ravdin found that two-thirds of the
Philadelphia physicians they surveyed infrequently or never disclosed the
diagnosis of terminal cancer [3]. Rennick in nationwide survey found that 22
per cent of physicians never told patients of incurable cancer and 62 per cent
sometimes informed the patient [4]. Oken found that 90 per cent of the
physicians surveyed at Michael Reese Hospital in Chicago indicated that they did

not tell terminal patients their diagnoses [5]. Finally, Caldwell and Mishara found that sixty of seventy-three physicians in a private Detroit hospital refused to be interviewed on their attitudes toward dying patients [6]. Of the thirteen actually interviewed only two admitted telling their patients of a terminal diagnosis. However, the low level of cooperation seems to make this study inadequate for drawing any conclusions.

On the other hand, a study more recent than these four failed to support Schulz and Aderman's conclusions. Rea et al. contacted 151 physicians from ten specialities [7]. Of these, 61 per cent felt that patient must be told of terminal illness regardless of the physical status, age, or life expectancy of the patient. They also found that while many physicians wanted to be honest with their patients, they often had anxiety over the ability of dying patients to cope with the news of impending death and ran into conflict with family members who did not wish the patient to be told of the terminal condition. In these matters, 37 per cent said they would primarily honor the wishes of the family, while 9 per cent claim they will tell the patient what he wants to know regardless of the family's decision. The remainder leave their options more or less open by coordinating with the family what the patient will be told.

The apparent contradiction between the studies quoted by Schulz and Aderman and the study by Rea et al. [7] might be explained by a change in attitude among physicians during the last decade. The three major studies cited by Schulz and Aderman [2] were published in 1953, 1960 and 1961, while the study by Rea et al. was published in 1975. The present study was, in part, directed toward exploring the extent of the possible changes in the behavior of physicians. If physicians have indeed changed, the present study should replicate Rea's findings with a different population. In addition, the present study wished to see to what extent physicians differed from other hospital personnel (nurses and chaplains) and from a non-hospital sample (college students).

The present study also investigated the views of physicians as compared to other hospital personnel and college students on sustaining life in terminal patients. Opinion is divided on what is appropriate care for terminally ill patients. Nevertheless, the American medical community is being pressured to develop guidelines for determining the care given to terminally ill patients. The Karen Anne Quinlan case dominated the national headlines for several weeks in 1976 [8]. *The New England Journal of Medicine* published a series of articles describing guidelines currently in use to aid physicians in choosing the appropriate treatment for terminal patients [9-11]. Some of the practices described are based on the distinction between active and passive euthanasia, a distinction endorsed by the House of Delegates of the American Medical Association. Rachels vigorously attacked this distinction as without moral justification and demonstrated that passive euthanasia can lead to great pain and suffering [12].

Indications of the changing national opinion on the issue of euthanasia are easy to find. In 1973, the *Gallup Opinion Index* reported that public approval of active euthanasia has increased sharply since 1950 [13]. A majority of Americans (53%) said that when a person has a disease which cannot be cured, doctors should be allowed by law to end that patient's life by some painless means if the patient and his family request it. In the 1950 survey only 36 per cent of Americans said they approved of active euthanasia. Rea et al. [7] did not ask their sample of physicians about active euthanasia; however, 68 per cent of their sample generally disapproved of extreme or heroic measures to keep terminal patients alive. The focus of the discussion about the critieria for sustaining life is also changing among moralists. McCormick, a leading Roman Catholic moralist, takes the position that technological advances and the sophistication of modern medicine increasingly obviate the need to consider the means, whether ordinary or extraordinary, to preserve life and place the judgmental burden on the reasonable hope of benefit for the patient [14]. In his view, quality of life—absence of excruciating or intractable pain and ability to experience, to relate, to communicate with fellow human beings—will replace other criteria used to judge the obligation to sustain life.

The Survey and the Respondents

Four identical surveys were conducted with physicians, nurses, chaplains, and college students. Utilizing four groups provided comparisons with physicians' attitudes from both within and without the hospital community. The questions on the survey are reproduced in Table 1 which includes the results. The surveys were conducted during October, 1976, at Lutheran General Hospital and at Loyola University of Chicago. For the purposes of the survey "terminal illness" was defined as "an illness that cannot be cured or controlled and that will most probably lead to a patient's death in a relatively short time (at most one year)."

A sample of staff physicians from the specialties of internal medicine, surgery, pediatrics, general practice, neurology, and oncology was contacted either by personal interview or by interoffice mail. Of thiry-five staff physicians contacted, twenty-nine (83%) responded. Five of the six staff physicians who did not respond were surgeons. Eighteen resident physicians were also contacted. Of these, sixteen (89%) cooperated. A sample of staff nurses on the medical and surgical units were also invited to fill out the questionnaires. Some nurses were contacted directly, others through their head nurse. Of these staff nurses, thirty (86%) cooperated. Twenty-six senior nursing students from the hospital nursing school were also contacted in their classroom. All of them cooperated. Of the staff chaplains contacted, sixteen (94%) filled out questionnaires, while all twelve of the student chaplains filled out questionnaires. Finally, ninety-seven freshman college students were approached in their psychology classes. All cooperated. The results, therefore,

Table 1. Responses to Terminal Illness Questionnaire Comparing
Physicians, Nurses, Chaplains, and College Students

Numbers Indicates Percentages	Physicians N = 45	Nurses N = 56	Chaplains N = 28	Students N = 97
1. If terminal patients request the information, do you feel they have an *unqualified* right to know the truth about their terminal conditions?				
% responding "yes"	87	86	79	81
2. Should a physician ever delegate the responsibility of informing the patient of his (her) terminal condition?				
Never	49	30	7	31
Rarely	51	52	79	47
Frequently	0	16	14	22
3. Who would you prefer to tell you, if you had a terminal illness?				
A physician	93	79	71	68
My spouse or nearest relative	4	7	7	21
My clergyman	2	4	7	3
No one	0	0	0	4
Other	0	7	14	4
4. What factors should ordinarily determine whether or not a patient is told of his (her) terminal condition?				
% responding "yes" to each item:				
Youth	44	46	25	57
Advanced age	31	32	21	46
Length of life expectancy	29	34	36	53
Emotional stability	71	86	71	93
Depth of religious faith	13	23	18	38
Emotional support from family	33	50	39	77

Table 1. (cont'd.)

Numbers Indicates Percentages	Physicians N = 45	Nurses N = 56	Chaplains N = 28	Students N = 97
5. As a general rule the physician should:				
a. give complete and honest information regarding the terminal condition without waiting for the patient to ask.	29	45	25	47
b. take the initiative in revealing the terminal condition, but then only answer specific questions the terminal patient asks.	42	43	50	26
c. answer completely and honestly the specific questions the terminal patient asks, but not take the initiative in revealing the terminal condition.	27	11	21	18
d. answer the patient's questions only to the extent the physician feels is appropriate.	2	2	4	9
6. Should a physician ever tell a patient about his (her) terminal condition against the wishes of the patient's spouse?				
% responding "yes"	84	88	93	71
7. Should the physician allow the terminal patient who is in acute pain to receive pain medication at the patient's request even though the drugs may hasten death?				
% responding "yes"	93	98	93	88

Table 1. (cont'd.)

Numbers Indicates Percentages	Physicians N = 45	Nurses N = 56	Chaplains N = 28	Students N = 97
8. Is is a physician's responsibility to keep a terminally ill patient alive even though extreme pain and financial hardship would be involved?				
% responding "yes"	20	21	4	41
9. Do you support "passive euthanasia," that is, using ordinary means of maintaining life but otherwise allowing nature to run its course with terminally ill patients?				
% responding "yes"	91	100	96	87
10. When a person has a disease that cannot be cured, do you think doctors should be allowed by law to end the patient's life by some painless means if the patient and his family request it?				
% responding "yes"	17	36	21	59
11. Do you feel that the "quality of life"—absence of excrutiating or intractable pain and the ability to experience, to relate, to communicate with fellow human beings—should replace all other criteria used to decide when to sustain life?				
Yes	36	36	25	29
No	31	18	39	22
Uncertain	33	43	32	53
NA	0	4	4	0
12. Age: Median	38	22	41	18

Table 1. (cont'd.)

Numbers Indicates Percentages	Physicians N = 45	Nurses N = 56	Chaplains N = 28	Students N = 97
13. Sex: Male	91	0	75	32
Female	9	100	25	68
14. Religious affiliation:				
Protestant	18	55	68	10
Catholic	20	32	29	80
Jewish	44	2	4	5
Other	11	4	0	4
No religious affiliation	7	5	0	0
15. Frequency of contact with terminal patients:				
1 or more times a month	74	73	69	0

are based on the responses of forty-five physicians, fifty-six nurses, twenty-eight chaplains, and ninety-seven college students. Few of the college students had any contact with terminally ill people. Over 73 per cent of the hospital personnel dealt with more than one terminally ill patient each month. The median ages and sexual composition of the four groups are given in Table 1 along with the religious affiliation of the respondents.

Results

INFORMING TERMINAL PATIENTS OF THEIR DIAGNOSES

The results of the survey are summarized in Table 1. The proportion of physicians (87%) who felt that patients have an unqualified right to know the truth if they request the information (Question 1), slightly but not significantly, exceeded the proportions of affirmative answers of the comparison groups. As for delegating their responsibility to inform the patient, physicians were less willing ($p < .05$)[1] to delegate responsibility than the other groups were willing to have physicians delegate this responsibility (Question 2).

None of the hospital personnel and only 4 per cent of the college students said that they did not want anyone to tell them if they had a terminal illness (Question 3). There was also consensus among all groups that the physician was the one to provide the information. The comparison groups, however, said more frequently than the physicians that they wanted a spouse or nearest relative to be the one to break the bad news ($p < .05$).

[1] All probabilities refer to two-tailed tests of the differences between two proportions.

As for the factors that should ordinarily determine whether or not a patient is told, there was a consensus among all groups that emotional stability was the most important factor to consider and that depth of religious faith was the least important factor (Question 4). Opinion was divided on the other factors. With respect to taking the initiative in telling a patient of his terminal condition (Question 5, statements "a" and "b"), 71 per cent of physicians said they should do so. An even greater proportion of nurses (88%) felt the physician should take the initiative to inform the patient ($p < .05$). Most of the physicians (84%) said that there were times when they should tell the patient against the wishes of the patient's spouse (Question 6). The situations when the spouse's wishes would be ignored were usually described as "when the patient asks" or "when the patient shows that he is emotionally ready to cope with the knowledge." Nurses and chaplains agreed with physicians on dealing with a spouse who wants to hide a terminal condition from the patient. The only comparison that approached statistical significance was between physicians (84%) and students (71%) who deferred slightly more to the family ($p < .10$) as they did on Question 3.

ATTITUDES ABOUT VARIOUS FORMS OF EUTHANASIA

The groups surveyed agreed that a terminal patient in pain should be permitted to request and receive pain medication even if the drugs may hasten death (Question 7). There were two questions dealing with *passive* euthanasia. These two different wordings led to somewhat different responses. Question 8 asked if a physician had a responsibility to keep terminally ill patients alive in spite of pain and financial hardship. Only 4 per cent of chaplains agreed with Question 8 compared to 20 per cent of physicians and 21 per cent of nurses ($p < .05$). However, more students (41%) agreed than the members of any other group ($p < .01$). The statement was rephrased into one that supported passive euthanasia (Question 9). All four groups (91% of physicians, 96% of chaplains, 87% of students and 100% of nurses) supported the idea of permitting "nature to run its course" after providing ordinary care to terminal patients. Regardless of which question is examined, hospital personnel largely agreed with the AMA's House of Delegates' endorsement of passive euthanasia. The college students were less consistent from Question 8 to Question 9; however, a majority on both questions agree with the hospital personnel in supporting passive euthanasia.

A majority of college students (59%) and student nurses (54%) endorsed *active* euthanasia (Question 10). By contrast, only 17 per cent of physicians, 21 per cent of chaplains and 20 per cent of staff nurses endorsed mercy killing. Each of these groups agreed less than the two student groups ($p < .05$). Thus, the findings of the 1973 Gallup poll were replicated in the sense that the youngest respondent groups (college students and student nurses) were much more favorable to euthanasia than were the older respondents. In contrast, the older respondents, all working in health care, reported euthanasia to be much less acceptable than similarly-aged respondents in Gallup's national sample.

The most controversial question in the survey was whether the "quality of life" should replace all other criteria used to decide when to sustain life (Question 10). Only about one-third of all four groups answered affirmatively to this question. Some reported they answered negatively because they did not feel that the quality of life should replace ALL other criteria, but should receive more importance than in the past. It was only on this question that staff and resident physicians differed markedly. While only 24 per cent of staff physicians felt that the quality of life should be the only important consideration in deciding when to sustain life, 56 per cent of the resident physicians did ($p < .05$).

Religion and sex of respondent did not prove to be important variables in this survey, nor were they important in the Gallup survey.

Discussion

This study supports the hypothesis that there has been a shift toward more openness among physicians over the last decade in informing terminal patients of their conditions. Physicians in the present sample were prepared to be even more open and frank with their terminally ill patients and their spouses than those interviewed by Rea et al. The attitudes of physicians in this study did not differ greatly from those of nurses, chaplains, and a non-hospital sample of college students concerning disclosing information to terminal patients. Of even greater importance was the deep concern and interest that the majority of physicians showed during the interviews regarding issues dealing with dying patients. Some interviews took twenty to thirty minutes because the physicians wished to elaborate and clarify their thinking for the interviewer. Many staff physicians emphasized that they considered the manner in which they informed their patients to be the most important consideration.

This study did not investigate whether physicians followed through on their convictions and actually informed their patients clearly without euphemisms or circumlocutions. However, results from another study at the same hospital revealed that 90 per cent of cancer patients who were supposed to have been told of their conditions indicated that they knew they were being treated for cancer.

With respect to sustaining life in terminal patients, there was almost unanimous support for *passive* euthanasia (i.e. not using extraordinary means) among all four groups of respondents. The groups would endorse the general thrust of the articles recently published in *The New England Journal of Medicine* which in essence described guidelines for administering programs of passive euthanasia [9-11].

On the other hand, while the majority of college students and student nurses endorsed *active* euthanasia (mercy killing), only about one-fifth of physicians, chaplains, and staff nurses endorsed active euthanasia. The survey itself does not provide any clues as to why hospital personnel differ from the general public on this issue. Is it because hospital personnel devote so much time and effort to preserving life that they cannot endorse actively participating in the ending of life? Or, do they recognize better than the younger and the non-hospital groups do that there would be great difficulties in administering a euthanasia policy? Or, do they reject it simply because they would be responsible for implementing any decisions that would result in mercy killings and/or would be associated with the institution responsible for these deaths? Perhaps it is easier to be for euthanasia when someone else actually is responsible for ending an ill person's life. The majority of hospital personnel, thus, do not seem uncomfortable in distinguishing between active and passive euthanasia. If the distinction is as untenable as Rachels maintains, the groups tested have not sensed the alleged logical inconsistency.

REFERENCES

1. E. Kübler-Ross, *On Death and Dying*, The MacMillan Company, New York, 1969.
2. R. Schulz and D. Aderman, Physicians and the Terminal Patient, *Omega*, *6:3*, pp. 291-302, 1975.
3. W. T. Fitts and I. S. Ravdin, What Philadelphia Physicians tell Patients with Cancer, *J. Amer. Med. Association*, *153*, pp. 901-904, 1953.
4. D. Rennick, What Should Physicians Tell Cancer Patients?, *New Med. Material*, pp. 51-53, 1969.
5. D. Oken, What to Tell Cancer Patients, *J. Amer. Med. Association*, *175*, pp. 86-94, 1961.
6. D. Caldwell and B. L. Mishara, Research on Attitudes of Medical Doctors Toward the Dying Patient, A Methodogical Problem, *Omega*, *3:4*, pp. 341-346, 1972.
7. M. P. Rea, S. Greenspoon and B. Spilka, Physicians and the Terminal Patient, *Omega*, *6:3*, pp. 291-302, 1975.
8. The Right to Die, *Time*, *108*, p. 101, October 11, 1976.
9. S. Bok, Personal Directions for Care at the End of Life, *New England J. of Med.*, *295*, pp. 367-369, 1976.
10. H. Pontoppidan, W. M. Abbott and D. C. Brewster, et al., Optimum Care for Hopelessly Ill Patients, *New England J. of Med.*, *295*, pp. 362-364, 1976.
11. M. T. Rabkin, G. Gillerman and N. R. Rice, Orders not to Resuscitate, *New England J. of Med.*, *195*, pp. 364-366, 1976.
12. J. Rachels, Active and Passive Euthanasia, *New England J. of Med.*, *292*, pp. 78-80, 1975.
13. Majority of Americans Now Say Doctors Should be Able to Practice Euthanasia, *The Gallup Opinion Index*, *98*, pp. 35-37, August, 1973.
14. R. A. McCormick, A Proposal for "Quality of Life" Criteria for Sustaining Life, *Hospital Progress*, *56*, pp. 76-79, September, 1975.